THE SCHWEICH LECTURES ON
BIBLICAL ARCHAEOLOGY, 1938

vol. 31.

THE WORK
OF THE CHRONICLER
ITS PURPOSE AND ITS DATE

THE WORK
OF THE CHRONICLER

ITS PURPOSE AND ITS DATE

BY

ADAM C. WELCH, D.D.

Emeritus Professor of Hebrew
and Old Testament Literature
New College, Edinburgh

THE SCHWEICH LECTURES
OF THE BRITISH ACADEMY
1938

LONDON
PUBLISHED FOR THE BRITISH ACADEMY
BY HUMPHREY MILFORD, OXFORD UNIVERSITY PRESS
AMEN HOUSE, E.C.
1939

PRINTED IN GREAT BRITAIN

PREFACE

THE author acknowledges the honour which the Schweich Trustees have conferred upon him by inviting him to become their lecturer. He acknowledges even more warmly the opportunity they have put within his reach of publishing a study on a somewhat neglected book, which, without their help, would never have seen the light. The chance to contribute something to the elucidation of a literature to which most of his working life has been devoted is more to the writer than any personal honour, high and highly valued though that is.

The lectures have been entirely recast in their new form. The time at the lecturer's disposal as well as the character of the audience made it necessary to present in the lectures no more than the author's results. In the present volume he has offered in full the evidence on which those results are based. Without the evidence the results would have been negligible to his fellow students.

It only remains to add that, after the Introduction, the symbols C and K are generally used for the Chronicler and for the author of Kings respectively; and that the Biblical references follow the numbering which appears in the Hebrew text.

CONTENTS

INTRODUCTION

IN an earlier series of lectures, delivered under the Baird Trust in Glasgow, the writer advanced the opinion that the nine chapters at the beginning of the books of Chronicles and the two verses which form their conclusion have no integral relation to the rest of the material, and have been added later.[1] The work of the Chronicler, therefore, which is the subject of the present study, is to be found in I Chr. 10: 1 —II Chr. 36: 21 and, when the alien elements have been removed, can be seen to present a definite unity. It dealt with the period of the kingdom in Judah from the time of its foundation by David to that of its collapse under Zedekiah.

Thus to define the scope of the Chronicler's work brings into the foreground the fact that his book covered the same ground which had already been traversed in part of Samuel and in the two books of Kings, except that the author ignored the existence of the northern kingdom. This inevitably raises the question of the reason which led a writer, living a generation or more later, to return to the history of the Davidic kingdom and to rewrite its record with such fullness of detail. A duplication of two narratives, which shows precisely the same features as here, is unexampled in the Old Testament. We are familiar with the phenomenon of parallel accounts in Scripture. There were once in circulation two accounts of the patriarchal period, which told how Israel came to be, and which ended with the event of the Exodus which gave the nation its distinctive character and its national consciousness.[2]

[1] The reasons for this judgement are to be found in my *Post-Exilic Judaism*, pp. 185 ff.

[2] This is written in full recognition of the value of the work of Volz and Rudolph, *Der Elohist als Erzähler — ein Irrweg der Pentateuch-Kritik*, which has recently thrown doubt on this conclusion. The authors have shown good cause for questioning whether it is legitimate to pronounce with confidence that the J and E documents can be separated with the

Those records told how the people, possessed of common traditions about their past, and sharing an experience which set them apart from the world, were prepared to meet the future. Again, what we can only infer about the patriarchal narratives is no matter of inference as to the history of the kingdom, for the compiler of the books of Kings has referred to the sources on which he drew, and has stated that he used material from the North Israelite and Judean archives. But these two cases of duplication differ in important aspects from that which engages our attention. Thus it is not hard to understand why, in the period when both branches were quickened into vigour and national consciousness by the institution of the kingdom, the desire was awakened to tell the story of how Israel came to be and to commemorate the men who helped to make it. Each produced its own version, which reproduced its peculiar traditions and glorified its own heroes. As naturally, each of the rival kingdoms preserved the records of its past in the Chronicles of the kings of Israel and Judah. In both instances, however, these separate narratives were combined in the form which we now possess; and, as it was possible to find a reason for their separate existence, it is equally possible to account for their amalgamation. With the disappearance of the northern kingdom Judah became the only representative of Israel, and, as it maintained all the hope for the future, so it inherited all

exactness which has been claimed for the process. They have also shown that too much reliance has been placed on differences of language, and even at times on the existence of narratives which were supposed to be duplicates. The criteria employed by criticism in its work of dissection have been too narrow in their character and were often too uncertain to bear out all the conclusions which have been based on them. The superstructure is top-heavy, and is crumbling because of the inadequacy of its foundations. But, in my judgement, their work has not succeeded in overturning the broad conclusion that there were once two parallel documents. The proof for this theory may have been inadequately stated and at times has been overstrained; but the theory itself meets too many difficulties and accounts for too many facts to be lightly discarded.

the traditions of the past. The men of that generation were seeking to restore the lost unity of Israel, and were using the bond of their common religion and of their common past to serve this end. They recognized that the continued existence of separate records of that past was worse than useless, since these brought a constant reminder of the old schism, the memory of which they were anxious to obliterate. The blending into one of the records of the two branches of the people was a part of that process of centralization which began after the fall of Samaria, and which is too narrowly construed when it is thought of as no more than the centralization of sacrificial worship at the temple. The single record of the past meant a reassertion of the unity of Israel. The situation, however, is different when we turn to the work of the Chronicler. Here we have an author who belonged to the reunited nation, and who was writing in and for the same community as that for which the author of Kings produced his book. Yet he rewrote the history of the kingdom, and was so conscious of the importance of what he did that he made his account as long as that of his predecessor. Also, though he added a good deal which dealt with the temple and the relation of the kings to the sanctuary, he did not put this into an appendix to Kings, but gave it a more appropriate setting in his own narrative, as though it could only be fully appreciated in its new connexion. Nor was any effort ever made to amalgamate the two records. It might appear as though men were conscious of a difference between the two which made such a step impracticable.

This feature of the book has not received much attention from those who have issued commentaries on Chronicles. Kittel in his commentary[1] was largely dominated by his interest as a historian. While it would be ungrateful to ignore the value of his notes on the chapters which deal with the temple and its arrangements, it remains true that his chief interest lay in determining the relative value of Kings and Chronicles as sources for providing material to the

[1] *Handkommentar zum A.T.*: Vandenhoeck und Rupprecht.

history of Israel. He compared with great care the parallel passages in the two books, and brought the acuteness and wide knowledge of a trained historian to bear on the question as to which supplied the more reliable information on the kingdom. His general conclusion was that, while in a few cases Chronicles might draw upon other sources than those which appeared in Kings, the author, as a rule, followed closely the account of his predecessor. Yet this decision only made it inevitable to ask why the Chronicler had taken the trouble to reproduce material which was more adequately set down already. Nor did Kittel fully realize the extent to which the later writer recast in certain cases the incidents which he borrowed, so that in his account they convey a wholly different view of the character of a king or of the connexion of events. This limitation is specially evident in connexion with the life of David and the course of Josiah's reformation.

Further, there is a considerable element in the Chronicler's work, which his commentator treated in a somewhat perfunctory fashion. He dismissed it with little consideration, calling it mere *midrash*, though he nowhere defined the precise meaning of that term. The reader was left to infer that the reason for this treatment of the passages was their want of value as a contribution to history. Yet the material is there, it is tolerably abundant in the document under review, and it is characteristic of that document, since none of it appears in Kings. It is somewhat cavalier treatment of an ancient book to measure its contents by the extent to which they conform to the standard laid down by a modern historian. Real recognition of this peculiar element in the book might have suggested that the Chronicler was not specially interested in history *qua* history, but was using that form of writing in order to convey his judgement on a period. The recognition of this possibility might in turn have explained why he added so little to the record which he took over from Kings, and why he recast some of the incidents in a way which suited his purpose.

The monumental commentary, which was begun by Rothstein and completed by Hänel,[1] was very different in character. Rothstein was convinced that the books of Chronicles were not homogeneous, and he set himself with infinite patience to trace the different hands which had contributed to give them their present form. He employed the methods which had been followed in the criticism of the Pentateuch, and relied greatly on the evidence of difference in language and on the presence of contradictions or parallels in the account. But the results were not very convincing, perhaps because scholars were beginning to become uneasy about the reliability of the results from the application of these methods in the earlier field. When one found a verse, which was merely introductory, assigned to three different hands, it was difficult to believe that any book had come into existence after this complicated fashion. The dissection might agree with Rothstein's criteria, but a reader could scarcely avoid the suspicion that criteria which compelled such conclusions were themselves doubtful. Nor was he reassured, when he attempted to discover why the original had been subjected to this elaborate series of revisions, for there did not appear to be any common outlook which gave unity to the notes or parallel material which had been so liberally introduced into the text. The annotations remained sporadic in character and a little haphazard in their additions to or corrections of the original, and showed no particular aim in the successive editors. One thing, however, the commentary has done; it has clearly proved that Chronicles is not derived from one hand, but has been subjected to a very thorough revision. But by accomplishing this, it has raised another and very pertinent question. Why has the Chronicler's work been so liberally annotated by later hands, while that of his predecessor in Kings has been left practically without correction? It might have been expected that the opposite would have been the case, and that the earlier book would have required a revision in order to bring it

[1] Sellin's *Kommentar*: Deichertsche Buchhandlung, Leipzig.

into agreement with the outlook and needs of a later time. There must have been some element in the Chronicler's treatment of his subject, which not only excited the interest, but roused the criticism of his contemporaries. What made this conclusion more sure was that the annotations were most frequent in the passages which were peculiar to the Chronicler, and were fewer and less important in the material which was common to him and the author of Kings.

This brief résumé of some recent work on Chronicles does not pretend to sum up all the contributions made to its interpretation, or to deal adequately with the special contribution of the two scholars cited. The present writer has chosen the two modern commentaries which best represent two leading lines of approach to the study of the book, and has indicated the results which in his view they have proved. But these results have left unanswered two questions relating to the book, which to him appear of primary importance— the reason which prompted the Chronicler to duplicate the history of the kingdom, and the reason for this account having received so much attention from revisers. This feeling of something which has not yet found an answer may form the excuse, if one be needed, for approaching the whole question along a different line. It is possible to ignore the demerits of the Chronicler as a historian, a subject which has been already dealt with by Kittel, and to concentrate attention on what the author had to say, and through the study of what he did say discover, if possible, the purpose he had in writing his book. In order to do this, it is necessary to bring an open mind and rigorously to refuse to determine beforehand what ought to have been in a history of Israel's kingdom, or to ignore anything which has been included there. Only after his narrative has been passed in review, is it legitimate to conclude his purpose in writing it.

For the sake of bringing some order into the study, it seemed advisable to group the material round certain large subjects. The first of these must be the life-work of David, were it only because the Chronicler devoted twenty chapters to the king's reign. But here the aim must be to discover the estimate he made of the character and work of the first king of Israel, and the place he assigned him in the life of the nation, and to recognize whether it differed from the picture which emerges in Kings. If any difference does emerge, it will be necessary to try to measure its significance. Any question of difference on historical matters between the two sources will only be of interest, so far as it has a bearing on the attitude which is assumed to David. The later writer may have departed from the course of events in Kings in order to make it bring out his peculiar view. The study of David will be followed by another on the series of prophets who are said in the second book to have appeared before certain kings to warn or to encourage them in the exercise of their functions. Because these incidents are supported by no other historical source, and are sometimes irreconcilable with the course of events in Kings, and because in themselves they are very difficult to accept as a record of events, they have been generally ignored. For this study they are of peculiar interest, even if they must be set down as a creation of the Chronicler. For they introduce the student directly to the author's mind and to his thought on such large questions as the function of prophecy and its relation to the kingdom. Above all, they throw light on his attitude to the kingdom and to the Davidic dynasty. Where the author of Kings judged the successive kings by whether they suppressed or maintained the high places, the Chronicler introduced a different standard, and measured their allegiance to Yahweh by their obedience to the divine message through the prophets.

Again, Chronicles is distinguished from Kings by the attention which its author devoted to the temple, its cult, and its clergy. He made David the real originator of the sanctuary, and reduced Solomon's share in the work to no more than the faithful carrying out of his father's plans. He further credited David with having organized the temple services and allotted their duties to the temple personnel.

In his description of these arrangements he brought into special prominence the levites, a body of clergy who are ignored in any reference which the author of Kings made to the temple. Two chapters have been devoted to this subject. The first deals directly with the major question of the status which is given to the levites throughout the book. The second is more limited in its character, for it is devoted to an analysis of a block of material which occupies the closing chapters in I Chronicles, and which purports to contain the instructions as to the arrangements in the future temple which David delivered to Solomon immediately before his death. These two chapters introduce, to a greater extent than before, the difficult and involved problem of the extent of the revision which the book has received and of the character of this revision. Cognate to this is the following discussion of Hezekiah's reform. Here, again, it may be necessary to insist that no attention need be given to the question as to whether the account of this reform is historically reliable. Even if it should be held that it is a free creation on the part of the Chronicler, the fact remains that he made Hezekiah, not Josiah, the originator of the great reform of religion which took place some time before the disappearance of the kingdom. The three chapters, therefore, in which he described this reform, present his idea of the lines on which such a reform ought to have been carried out and his conception of the conduct which befitted a reforming king. The closing chapter is occupied with a discussion of the relation between the Chronicler and Deuteronomy, which falls a little out of line with what has preceded. It cannot, however, be omitted in any study on the book, were it only for the light it casts on the question of its date.

The line of approach to Chronicles which has thus been indicated may supplement the work of Kittel and Rothstein. On the one hand, it will bring into the foreground the elements in the book which Kittel was inclined to brush aside, and, by giving them a due place, may suggest that its author had another purpose in view than that of writing history. On the other hand, it will concentrate attention on the different attitude which emerges in the original narrative and in the annotations, and so may suggest a reason for Chronicles having received an amount of revision which is absent from Kings.

I

DAVID IN THE BOOK OF CHRONICLES

THE importance of the role which C assigned to David appears from the fact that twenty chapters out of the fifty-six of which his book is composed were devoted to the life of the king. Of these twenty chapters, also, more than half are peculiar to the later record, and have no parallel in the Book of Samuel or that of Kings. We are thus exceptionally well supplied with information on the position which was given to David there. For we are not dependent on conclusions drawn from the passages which C omitted or from the changes he made in those which he included. These might mislead a student, since he must in both cases supply his own reasons for the departure from the original, and, in so doing, might follow his own ideas and go widely astray. But the chapters which have been added represent C's independent point of view, and give his reasons for attaching so much importance to the early reign. A student is thus supplied with a clue which may guide him in his attempt to determine the reason which prompted both the omissions and the alterations which were made in the earlier narrative.

C then began his narrative with the accession of David as King over united Israel. He prefaced the account by the story of Saul's defeat on Mt. Gilboa, I Chr. c. 10, which he based on I Sam. c. 31. But the changes which he introduced and the new setting in which he placed the story gave the whole a different aspect.

The author of Samuel set the defeat at Gilboa in its historical perspective. On the one hand, he made it the final incident in Saul's lifelong struggle with the Philistines. On the other hand, he made it no more than the first stage in the accession of the new king. David must settle with Saul's house in the person of Ishbaal, and only after the collapse of that ill-starred kinglet was he able to transform his kingdom over Judah at Hebron into one over all Israel at Jerusalem. After Ishbaal's death the elders of Israel transferred their allegiance to the new king. But to the end of his reign David must reckon with the fact that the older line had its supporters in the kingdom. The Rizpah incident and the attitude of Shimei and Meribaal at the time of Absalom's rebellion proved that there was a party in Israel which counted him a usurper.

The attitude of C to the defeat at Gilboa appears in the two verses which he added to the story, vv. 13f. That disaster was no mere incident in the war with the Philistines: in it the divine judgement was pronounced on the early kingdom. Saul died for his trespass against the word of the Lord. Therefore the Lord slew him, and brought his dynasty as well as himself to an end. There could be no successor to the doomed house, for, when Saul died with his three sons, all his house died together, v. 6.[1] Accordingly, C omitted all mention of the kingdom of Ishbaal and of David's temporary reign at Hebron. He was equally silent about the incidents in David's reign which proved the existence of a constant and formidable opposition in the interest of Saul's house.[2] Instead of making the elders of Israel wait until Ishbaal was dead before they came to Hebron with the offer of the crown, he made their act immediately follow Gilboa. The men recognized in that débâcle the divine decision, for they did not merely anoint David to be king as in Samuel, they anointed him according to the word of the Lord by the hand of Samuel, 11: 3. The new king did not come to the throne, because the leaders of Israel recognized in him the only man who was competent to meet the situation in which their

---

[1] Incidentally, it may be noted that the inclusion of a genealogy of Saul at I Chr. 8: 33–40, since it contradicts the statement here, is an additional proof that the early nine chapters were no integral part of the work of C.

[2] The only place at which occurs a reference to the Hebron kingdom is I Chr. 29: 27, which is a verbatim copy of the summary of the reign from K. It is not surprising that this casual reference was overlooked.

nation stood. He owed his dignity to the divine choice, in which the entire nation at once and unanimously acquiesced.

Immediately after his accession the king marched against and captured Jerusalem.[1] Here C followed the account of his predecessor. He omitted, however, the summary of the reign which prefaced that account: it contained the unwelcome reference to the temporary kingdom at Hebron. Instead, also, of crediting the capture of the new capital to David and his men, as in 5: 6, he ascribed the feat to David and all Israel, 11 : 4. The centre for the kingdom, the future centre for the worship of the people, had been won by no privately enlisted troops, but by the united nation with its king at its head. C further made David promise the dignity of Commander-in-Chief of the army to the first man who entered the fortress, and told how Joab won the coveted honour through his courage. Now, according to Samuel, Joab had been Commander-in-Chief during the years at Hebron, and had risked a blood feud in order to prevent an Israelite from supplanting him. The leader of Israel's army must owe his appointment to its king.

As soon as Jerusalem was won, C continued to insist on the unanimity with which the entire nation had accepted its new ruler. The author of Samuel had either written or preserved a list of the names of mighty men in the army with incidents which related how some of these had won distinction. The list, however, appears in an appendix to the reign, II Sam. 23: 8 ff. Because of the place where it appears, it is not possible to pronounce whether it was the work of the historian, or an addition by an editor. Neither is it easy to determine the period or periods in David's life to which the incidents to which it alludes must be referred. C brought the list out of its original place in an appendix, and has referred them all to the years which preceded the accession, 11 : 10-47. Even then, before he reached the throne, men of such quality, who derived from more than Judah, had been among his followers. For C prefaced the list with a

[1] I Chr. 11: 4–9, cf. II Sam. 5: 4–10.

statement, which both gave his reason for inserting it where he did, and dwelt on the quality which marked all the men, whatever might be the special distinction of individuals among them. These men 'showed themselves strong with him in his kingdom, together with all Israel, to make him king, according to the word of the Lord concerning Israel', 11 : 10. The representatives of the nation and its bravest had combined in supporting the king, and, in doing so, acquiesced in a greater purpose than their own.

This list was followed by another series of names and numbers of a similar character in chap. 12. The additional list falls naturally into two sections, vv. 1–22 and vv. 23–40, which differ in one particular. The earlier verses state that contingents from certain tribes joined David during the period which preceded his accession: the later profess to give the numbers of those who came from the several tribes in order to take part in his election to the throne. The source of these passages is quite uncertain; indeed it is an open question whether the Chronicler drew on any original,[1] or gave free rein to his own imagination. It has always appeared to me more probable that much of the material in vv. 1–23 derives from earlier sources. Evidently the period of David's flight before Saul appealed very strongly to the imagination of the early Hebrews, as the number of such folk tales collected by the author of Samuel is enough to prove. Stories about the hunted fugitive who rose to high honour have always exercised a romantic appeal; and, when the hero not only became king but succeeded in restoring the unity and independence of his kingdom, they have a long life. The vividness of the two incidents which are related about the Gadites and about Amasai suggests a very different type of mind from that of C, who had a rather heavy hand when he attempted to restore the past. He may have selected material from an unknown source to complete his picture of David.

---

[1] Curtis, e.g., in the I.C.C. Commentary has no hesitation in declaring most of the material to be a free creation, which may be dated at the period of the Return.

Then it becomes legitimate to note that the two incidents, which are most unlike his own style, served his purpose. For he thus brought out clearly that the men who came over to David in his early years were of fine quality and character. Again, when the young leader naturally showed some suspicion at the appearance of men from Benjamin, the tribe of Saul, their head claimed to be guided by divine inspiration. The men who supported the future king in his early years were not the broken men whom the author of Samuel described, I Sam. 22: 1–2. Nor were they so few in number as the 400 of I Sam. 22: 2, or the 600 of 27: 2: even before his accession David was at the head of a great host, like the host of God. Already also some of them, and among those men from Benjamin, were able and willing to acknowledge his divinely guided destiny.

The later section, vv. 24 ff, is different in character. It is so confused that it does not seem to be homogeneous; it also bears more evident signs of the style of C. It may, therefore, be a very free reconstruction on his part. But, however this may be, its general aim is unmistakable. The contingents which came to Hebron were drawn from all the tribes of Israel, and they were so numerous as to prove the unanimity of the nation in the nomination of the new king.

Immediately after the capture of Jerusalem, David set on foot the transference of the ark from the house of Obed-Edom. The new capital must become the religious centre of the nation. Here, as Kittel has remarked, C has departed from the order of events in the book of Samuel. In the earlier record the capture of Jerusalem was followed by the building of a palace, by a record of the royal family, and by the account of certain wars with the Philistines. Only then did the king find time to turn his attention to the ark. In C the conquest of the new capital was immediately followed by the effort to bring the sacred emblem into its shrine there. So pious an act could not have been delayed.

The story of the abortive attempt to bring up the ark in chap. 13 is, so far as the later part, vv. 6 ff., is concerned,

parallel to II Sam. 6 : 1–11, but it is prefaced by a short
introduction which is peculiar to C. The author of Samuel
made the king summon 30,000 leading men in Israel, at
whose head he went down to the house of Obed-Edom.
In C, on the other hand, when David convoked the captains
of thousands and the captains of hundreds, he did so in order
to lay before them the proposal that all Israel should be
brought together that they might take part in the solemn
act. In particular, he proposed to send messages to 'all our
brethren who are left in all the lands of Israel'. The result
was that the entire nation from the brook of Egypt to the
entering in of Hamath was assembled. Accordingly, while
the author of Samuel said that David went and all the
people who were with him, C changed this into David
and all Israel. The ark, which was to become the centre
for the worship of Israel, must be brought to its shrine in
Jerusalem by the united nation. It had been ignored
during the reign of the king whom God had rejected: one
of the earliest acts of the king whom God had chosen was
to give it fitting reverence, and to set it in its place at the
national shrine.

In these respects the passage continues the leading motif
which dominated C's conception of David and his work.
Under him Israel became a united kingdom, and now under
him it became one through the possession of a common
sanctuary. But the form of the proposal for effecting this
which the king is said to have brought before his leading
men is very peculiar in its character. It is already singular
to find him feeling the need specially to notify Israel proper
of the event: it is more singular to recognize the terms in
which this was to be done. The men are called our brethren;
they are described as those who are left in the lands of Israel;
they are said to have among them the priests and levites,
where all the LXX MSS. omit the *waw* and read the
'levitical priests'. Now the expression הנשארים, 'those who
are left in the *lands* of Israel', is peculiar to the post-exilic
literature, and is employed there to describe the men of the

North who survived the divine judgement in the exile under Sargon.[1] The natural explanation for the use of such language in David's time is to suppose that the author lapsed *per incuriam* into the phraseology of his own time. Was it a mere lapse? It remains a remarkable fact that the same author ascribed to Hezekiah and Josiah, the two later reforming kings who restored the conditions which prevailed under David, an equal anxiety that the same men, the remanent Israelites, should take part in the passover celebration at the restored temple. From him we learn of the messages Hezekiah dispatched for this purpose into the North. C was writing in view of the situation which prevailed in his own time. He chose the language which he did and put it into the mouth of David in order to express his conviction. Israel had an equal right with Judah in the worship at the temple. The king who instituted the national shrine at Jerusalem had deliberately included the men of the North in the initial act which made that shrine national. He had put the matter before the leaders of the people, and they had acquiesced in the proposal. For the remanent Israelites were the brethren of the men of Judah, and were treated as such.

This interpretation throws light upon another phrase in the proposal. As the sentence reads in the MT, the remark that the Israelites possessed priests and levites has no very appropriate meaning in itself and has no relation to the matter in hand. There is no obvious connexion between the statement that the Israelites had these two classes of clergy and David's desire to invite them to the ceremony of the transference of the ark. The meaning becomes much clearer, if we follow the unanimous Septuagint reading and understand a reference to the levitical priests. For that is the title applied to the priests of north Israel in Deuteronomy. When C put into David's mouth a reference to the priests of Israel, and when he connected this with an urgent request that the Israelites should take part in the inauguration of the temple,

[1] Cf. my *Post-Exilic Judaism*, pp. 59 ff.

D

he expressed his attitude to one of the burning questions of the time of the Return. The remanent Israelites had the privilege of sharing in the national worship on an equal footing with their Judean 'brethren', and their priests had a similar place in the cult-practice.

After the unsuccessful effort to transfer the ark, David, according to C, made careful arrangements in order to prevent a repetition. He prepared a מקום or shrine for the reception of the sacred emblem, and set up a tent in which it was to be lodged, 15 : 1. Pronouncing that only the levites were competent to act as its porters, he instructed the heads of fathers' houses of Levi to prepare themselves and to carry out the task, 15: 2, 12. When these measures proved successful and the ark was safely lodged with due honour in its new position, the king appointed certain levites to minister before it, 16: 4. This ministration implied more than the chanting of psalms at the new shrine, though a psalm, which was judged suitable for the occasion, has been included. For, at the first stage of its journey from the house of Obed Edom, sacrifices were offered before the emblem, 15 : 25 f.[1] Again, when David gave his final charge to Solomon as to the building of the temple, he commanded him to build the sanctuary of the Lord in order to 'bring the ark of the covenant of the Lord, and the holy vessels of God, into the house that is to be built to the name of the Lord', I Chr. 22:19. Now these vessels were more than musical instruments; they were employed for the cult. Accordingly, it is stated that, as soon as Solomon had fulfilled this command, and lodged the ark in its final resting-place, sacrifices were offered before it, II Chr. 5: 6. The ark was thus the centre of a regular cult, so that, according to C, the first shrine in

[1] The statement there does not *necessarily* imply that these sacrifices were offered by the levites. They were offered in recognition of the divine approval of the undertaking—when the Lord helped the levites who bare the ark of the covenant. But, when the verse continues ויזבחו or 'then they sacrificed', the verb may be used in the impersonal sense and may imply no more than that sacrifices were offered.

Jerusalem was that of Israel's ancient and revered palladium with the levites acting as its ministers.

The account of David's desire to build the temple with its rejection by Nathan appears in almost identical terms in the two sources.[1] The author of Samuel may have shown a certain dislike on the part of the prophet to the idea of any temple, since he dwelt on the fact that no such building had existed in Israel during the years in the wilderness or during the period of the judges. While C retained the historical references, he softened the refusal by changing the first clause of his predecessor, 'shalt thou build a house for me to dwell in' into 'not thou shalt build'. The earlier narrative took the edge off absolute rejection by inserting the later statement that Solomon was to fulfil the plan of his father; the later went a little further and included this assurance in the actual terms of the rejection. But the leading themes of the pericope were identical in the two historians. On the one hand, the founder of the future temple in purpose, if not in fact, was David. His design was to provide for the ark a more fitting shrine than the one which he had prepared for it at first. He desired to place it in surroundings which were more worthy of its position in the national life and of Him who was worshipped there. The temple was to take the place of the tent which had hitherto housed the ark. On the other hand, no less important was the other theme that, while David was forbidden to build a house for Yahweh, Yahweh purposed to build a house for David. The new king, who had come to the throne through the divine election, was to be the founder of a dynasty which equally owed its being to the divine will. If it realized the purpose to which it thus owed its existence, it would be made secure and enduring.[2]

---

[1] I Chr. c. 17, and II Sam. c. 7.

[2] The point would be made even more clear, if a slight emendation were made in 17 : 10. In its present form the text is more than awkward, since it implies a confused transition between Yahweh and the prophet as speakers. Rothstein has adopted an older suggestion that the divine name at the end of the verse is due to the error of the copyist, who read

The three following chapters, chaps. 18–20, which contain the account of David's wars, are largely extracted from the much longer record in the book of Samuel. The questions which they raise deal rather with points of detail and are not very relevant to the present study. Some are textual, others are concerned with the extent to which the Chronicler was dependent on other sources than those appearing in Samuel. The leading feature in the narrative of C, however, is the extent to which he has cut down the material which was at his command. As has been already stated, it is possible to suggest reasons for several of his omissions. He ignored David's dealings with Meribaal and his surrender of some of Saul's descendants to the Gibeonites, since all the house of Saul, according to his view, had fallen at Gilboa. He equally ignored the record of Absalom's rebellion, because it did not conform with his picture of the unity of the nation under its first king. His omission of the betrayal and murder of Uriah may have had a double motive. Not only did the story cast an ugly shadow on the fair fame of David, but it offered a singularly unfitting prelude to his representation of Solomon's accession. All the palace intrigues which brought Solomon to the throne disappeared from his account. In its place came a gathering of the leading men in Israel, to whom the old king presented his successor in the character of the one whom God had chosen. David had received the promise that his dynasty was sure of the divine blessing and support. It was not easy to bring this conception of the kingdom of Israel into agreement with the fact that David's successor was born in adultery.

יהוה instead of the והיה at the beginning of v. 11. This blunder brought about the change of an original אבנה I will build into יבנה, He, i.e. Yahweh, will build. I suggest that we should further read with the LXX וַאֲגַדֶּלְךָ in place of וְאַגִּד לְךָ, and translate the sentence—'I will subdue all thine enemies and will make thee great and I will build thee a house'. The effect of the change will be, not merely to remove the confusion between the speakers, but to make the contrast clearer. As God had given no command to the people in the past about a temple, but had appointed a place for Israel, so will He deal with David.

But all these omissions on the part of the Chronicler, whether it is possible or not to be sure as to the motives which prompted them, make one fact clear. They must be weighed along with the other fact of the additions which he introduced. He included everything from his source which bore upon the king's service to the nation in founding and strengthening the outward institutions of religion in Israel, and everything which he added went to prove that he was the originator of the temple and of the cult which was practised there. But he cut down severely the details of the royal wars and of all the means by which David built up a powerful kingdom.

Accordingly, after his brief mention of the wars in which David was engaged, the historian turned back to his favourite theme. Though the king had been forbidden personally to build the temple, he was to all intents and purposes its originator, for he collected materials for the purpose, arranged as to the workmen, designed the actual building, and determined the functions of the clergy who carried out the cult in it. These matters fill the remaining chapters of the first book of Chronicles. As the last thoughts and energies of the king were devoted to this great purpose of his life, so the last scene, when he was old and full of years, revealed him gathering the notables of the kingdom round him. He announced Solomon as his successor, and, as soon as his son was anointed, solemnly charged the new king and his people to carry out the work which he had begun. The leaders accepted their new ruler and showed their willingness to undertake the responsibility which had been laid upon them by contributing liberally to the preparations for the temple. As David's first task after his accession and conquest of Jerusalem had been to bring the ark into its shrine in the capital, so his dying charge to his successor was to guarantee the completion of the task by building the temple and bringing the ark and its vessels into it.

Most of this material, chaps. 22–9, is peculiar to the Chronicler, and, with slight exceptions, finds no parallel in

Samuel. But C prefaced it by the account of David's numbering of the people with the resultant pestilence, and the building of the altar on the threshing-floor of Araunah. This, his chap. 21, he took from II Sam. c. 24, following very closely his original. Yet he gave it an entirely new meaning through the position in which he set it, and through the slight changes he introduced into its terms.

In Samuel the story has been relegated to an appendix and appears among some other varied material which belonged to David's reign: it is not prominent in that reign, nor is it integrally related to the king's activity. Thus it opens with the statement that again the anger of the Lord was kindled against Israel, and He moved David to number the people. Evidently then the story was originally connected with another passage which related a previous outbreak of the divine anger. In my judgement it was so connected with the famine of chap. 21, which led to the deliverance of a number of Saul's descendants to the Gibeonites. When the men whom Saul had wronged had sacrificed those victims before the Lord, the rain which fell on Rizpah during her dreadful watch intimated that the atonement had been sufficient. Again the wrath of the Lord was kindled against Israel, but this time the offender was David himself. To stay the pestilence which resulted from the numbering of the people an altar was built on Mt. Zion and a sacrifice after the use of Israel was offered on it. The effect in both cases was the same: at Gibeon God was entreated for the land, at Mt. Zion the Lord was entreated for the land and the plague was stayed from Israel. It is possible that one reason for setting the two incidents in such close relation was to underline the different methods of atonement which were employed in Gibeon and in Israel, and so to counter the dangerous theological suggestion in the earlier story. It is even possible that this explains the different divine names which appear in the two accounts. God might be entreated by the methods which were followed by the semi-pagan remnant of the Amorites: Yahweh was entreated by a sacrifice which was after His mind. But, however this may be, the altar on Mt. Zion, according to the author of Samuel, had no permanent place in the national life. It had been erected to serve a special purpose, and, when that purpose was fulfilled, it need never have been used again.

C changed the entire character of the account, when he brought it out of the appendix to which his predecessor had relegated it, and set it in the main stream of his record of the reign. It was thus placed in integral relation to the leading purpose of David's life, instead of being connected with a similar visitation which had befallen the nation. For it followed the divine promise that, though David was forbidden to build the temple, his son was to be granted that privilege, and it preceded the ample preparations which were made to that end. How closely the succession of these events was linked together in his mind C made clear by the new conclusion which he added to his version of the story in 22:1. After the descent of the divine fire at the threshing-floor, which manifested the divine approval of the offering made on its altar, he put into David's mouth the solemn declaration: this is the house of the Lord God, and this the altar of burnt-offering for Israel. The altar on Mt. Zion was no temporary place of sacrifice, which served its purpose and ceased to have any further place in the national life: it had received a permanent consecration. Before the king made any preparations for the future temple, he received a divine revelation as to the site of the altar before which it must be built. C transformed the story which had told of David's sin in numbering his people, of its chastisement, of the king's repentance, and his atoning sacrifice: he made it into the ἱερὸς λόγος of the temple.

The minor changes which appear in the chapter bear the characteristic marks of C's style, and help to bring out his purpose. In v. 1 David numbered Israel, in Samuel, Judah and Israel; the total reported in v. 5a[1] was for all Israel, in

---

[1] Verse 5b, which is absent from the LXX, is recognized to be a gloss by Rothstein and even by Curtis.

Samuel the totals for Judah and Israel were set down separately. C thought of the nation as a unity when he described the origin of the sanctuary which was to serve it all. The angel commanded Gad to direct the building of the new altar, v. 18; the author of Samuel had been content to ascribe this command to the prophet. The altar which was to be the centre for sacrificial worship must have its site indicated by a direct divine command. When David purchased the threshing-floor, he used about it the technical term מקום or shrine at v. 25: contrast the language in Samuel, 24: 24. But above all C alone described how God accepted the sacrifice and hallowed the altar by sending down fire from heaven, v. 26b.[1]

As soon as the site of the future temple had been determined, David could press on his preparations, which he did abundantly, 22: 2–5. He then summoned Solomon, who was not yet his successor, and, giving a brief résumé of the reasons why he himself was not permitted to complete the work, he added that the great task had been reserved for his son. He therefore delivered over the preparations which he had made to Solomon and charged him with the responsibility of carrying them to completion, 22: 6–19. While the passage is peculiar to C, it contains certain echoes from the work of Kings. Thus the levy of workmen appears in I Kings 5: 27 f., v. 7 occurs almost verbatim in Solomon's prayer of dedication, I Kings 8: 17, the description of Solomon as a man of peace closely resembles the statement in I Kings 5: 4b, 18. It will be noted that these references are all to events which took place during the later reign. It was natural for C to introduce them here, because he credited David with everything connected with the temple, except the actual building. He made Solomon no more than the executant of the plans of his father.

Otherwise the chapter shows the characteristic attitude of its author. Since he was writing here with greater independence, he introduced, as the reason for David's inability

[1] On v. 29 f., see *infra*, p. 31 f.

to complete the temple, the fact that in his wars he had shed much blood. He returned to the same theme at 28: 3. On the other hand, where he followed his original more closely in the story of the prophet Nathan at chap. 17, he gave no such reason. Here, again, he may be borrowing from and expanding the work of his predecessor. For, in his account of Solomon, K referred to David's wars having interfered with the other sacred task, I Kings 5: 17; but, as Kittel recognized, this implied no more than that the constant wars did not leave the king leisure to undertake the task. As C supplemented K on this point, he also corrected him on another. K made Solomon raise his labour-levy for the work on the temple from all Israel, I Kings 5: 27 ff. According to C, David laid the corvée on the גֵרִים or strangers, cf. II Chr. 2: 16. Now these men, according to him, were the descendants of the original inhabitants of Palestine, II Chr. 8: 7 ff.[1]

The final charge, however, which David laid upon his son in connexion with the future temple is most significant as to the attitude of C. As soon as the temple was complete, Solomon must bring into it the ark of the covenant of the Lord and the sacred vessels of God. As to these sacred vessels, even Rothstein, though he referred to I Kings 8: 4, recognized their obvious association with the ark and its sanctuary. The new sanctuary must fulfil David's intention, when he desired a more worthy resting-place for the ark than the curtains of its tent. The temple was a substitute for that tent, and Solomon's first act, when the house of God was complete, must be to lodge in it the ark with the sacred vessels employed in its cult.[2]

[1] The later view of the situation has been introduced into the narrative of K as I Kings 9: 20–2.

[2] David's address to Solomon is followed by five chapters, 23–7. This block of material is the most confused and difficult section to unravel, even in the book of Chronicles. It is also very plainly not homogeneous in character; at least two writers, probably more, can be traced in its composition. The subject with which it chiefly deals is the way in which David determined the functions and the courses of the clergy in the future temple. I propose to deal with that large

The private charge of David to his son was followed by a public assembly, in which the old king resigned his throne and presented Solomon as his successor. He then reminded the notables of Israel that the chief task which lay upon the new king was that of building the Temple. After delivering to Solomon the תבנית or plan which he himself had prepared for the sanctuary and the treasures which he had accumulated, he reminded the leaders that their king would need all the help which they could give him in such a weighty undertaking, and called upon them to show their interest in it by contributing to meet the cost. When they gave a ready response to his appeal, he offered a humble thanksgiving to God and besought the divine blessing on the work which had been denied to him.

The relation between the two speeches has given occasion for a good deal of discussion. Rothstein and Benzinger were of opinion that chap. 28 was originally connected with 23: 1 f., and that the speech was delivered to that assembly of the leaders of Israel. With this judgement I agree, and merely add that the lengthy and pompous introduction in 28: 1 was added after chaps. 23–7 had been brought into their present position. Then the two speeches may both be retained, since one was addressed to Solomon in private before his accession and the other was delivered in public and was followed by the anointing of the new king. Kittel, however, judged it necessary to telescope the two speeches which he then redivided and referred to two separate authors. It is unnecessary to give the details of the division here, and it may be enough to say that by it the more precise description of the Temple, its furniture, and its officials was assigned to one writer, while the hortatory passages were allotted to another. Yet the two subjects are too closely interwoven,

topic at a later stage, and therefore pass over it here. When it comes to be reviewed, it will be necessary to attempt to decide how much of the contents of those chapters may be assigned to the Chronicler. Meantime all that can be assumed about them is that they prove C to have ascribed to David a judgement as to those clergy.

both in the text and in the thought, to admit of this dissection. A writer, who believed that the plan of the temple
and its arrangements had been divinely revealed to David,
must have counted the king's eagerness to commit this to his
successor an evidence of spiritual fervour. Further, whoever
this writer may have been, he lived during the time which
followed the Return, and so belonged to a generation which
judged the maintenance of the temple and its cult to be a
matter of life and death for the religion of their nation.

The objection which Kittel and some other students have
shown to accepting two speeches of very similar character,
as having been put into the mouth of David at the end of his
reign by the same writer, fails also to recognize one feature
which marks the public address. For the speech to the
leaders of Israel served two purposes. So far as it dwelt on
the supreme duty of building the temple, it covered much
the same ground as the private charge given by the king to
his son. But it was also intended to give C's view of the
accession of Solomon. We must read the account in its
relation to the discreditable version in Kings of the method
by which the new king succeeded in reaching the throne.
Then, and only then, does it become clear why, in addressing
the notables, David began by dwelling on two themes. He
spoke of the divine promise as to his dynasty in Israel, and
he put forward Solomon as his divinely elected successor.
In view of these commanding facts, the new king was at
once accepted by the leaders of the nation, and his accession
to the throne followed without opposition and as a matter of
course. As Israel elected David, because God had already
chosen him, so Israel elected his son.

The final charges delivered by David to his successor and
to his people contain an epitome of the Chronicler's judgement on the life-work of the first king of Israel. David had
united the nation under his authority and maintained that
unity throughout his reign. He had also been the founder
of the dynasty, which continued so long as the independence
of the nation lasted. He was able to accomplish these things

because in them he was the servant of a greater purpose than his own. God had chosen him and had rejected Saul; God had promised to grant him a house; God had chosen from among his many sons the one who was to succeed him. But the dynasty had failed to fulfil the divine purpose which had brought it into being,[1] and had therefore come to an inglorious end. A like failure, however, had not attended the other side of the first king's service to Israel. For he had laid the foundations for the temple, which was to be the centre of worship of Israel, and was to make Mt. Zion a praise to the ends of the earth. He set up the first sanctuary in Jerusalem when he brought up the ark and made it the centre of a cult. He conceived the purpose of building the temple which was to be its fitting shrine instead of its curtains. He planned the lines for its future buildings, and appointed the men who were to conduct its cult. David was, in everything except the actual physical labour, the originator of the temple; and in all he undertook for its future glory he was guided by God who had chosen him to be king. The site for the temple was indicated by a theophany, and the first sacrifice on its altar was consumed by a fire from heaven. The plan for the future buildings and for the officials there was given in writing from the hand of the Lord, 28: 19. Therefore he delivered it to the leaders of the nation, as the pattern for their future work. But he also charged Solomon to bring the ark of the covenant of the Lord and its sacred vessels into the completed temple, 22: 19, and he reminded the leaders of the nation that his design from the beginning had been to build a house of rest for the ark of the covenant of the Lord, 28: 2. Unless that sacred emblem with the vessels which belonged to its cult was housed in the new sanctuary, his purpose would be left incomplete. Because the king was thus the originator of the temple, it is said of the later kings who reformed the religion of the nation that they restored the conditions which had been laid down by David.

From this sketch of the Chronicler's account of David's

[1] On this subject cf. the later chapter on C's attitude to prophecy.

life, it is evident that he was not writing history in the sense in which we conceive that history ought to be written. He was using the records of his nation in order to convey certain theological teaching and to insist on certain ecclesiastical convictions. His work may be compared with that of the man or men who produced the account of Israel's origin, which dealt with the lives of the patriarchs. In certain respects C's work does not bear comparison with that of his predecessor. The two records have nothing in common when they are thought of as literature. The Chronicler had not the same imagination, the power of sketching character, the ability to make the past live. All that in these respects can be set down in his favour is that he probably reproduced with greater accuracy the facts with which he dealt in his narrative. He was not so free in his reproduction of the national past. But the aim of both writers was the same. They were using the material which they borrowed in order to impress certain great convictions on the mind of their contemporaries. Through C's account of David's life we can hear an authentic voice speaking from the period after the Return. What he had it in his heart to say was that David gave Israel two great gifts, the kingdom and the temple, the two institutions which dominated and coloured the national life in Palestine. The one had gone down the wind and could never return. It was conditioned by faithfulness on the part of its kings to the purpose which brought it into being. When the kings failed to obey God's voice through His prophets, the kingdom was doomed. But David's other gift of the temple remained, and in it and its worship was the hope for the future of Israel.

The temple, however, which David had planned, was, as has been pointed out, the substitute for the tent in which the ark had been housed. Even before it was built there had been a sanctuary of the Lord in Jerusalem, and a cult had been practised there which was valid for Israel. That had been the king's first care after the capture of his new capital. His last care had been that Solomon must transfer that cult to the temple when it was completed. Now in contrast with this leading theme which appears in each successive stage of David's conduct in relation to the national worship, it must be noted that there appears a different attitude in the course of the book. It must also be noted that the evidence of this different attitude emerges at the critical stages of the story. Thus, at the time when David brought the ark to Jerusalem and instituted a cult before it, appears the statement that Zadok the priest and his brethren the priests were before the tabernacle of the Lord in the high place at Gibeon to offer burnt-offerings unto the Lord upon the altar of burnt-offering continually morning and evening, 16: 39 f. The statement is not woven into the passage of which it forms part, but is abruptly interjected, having no connexion with what precedes or with what follows.

It is easy to understand why David honoured the ark, which had played a part in the wilderness journeys and had already been the centre of a cult at Shiloh. It is not easy to explain why the tabernacle, which was a dominant feature in those journeys, disappeared from the life of the nation after they reached Palestine, and why, when it suddenly reappears, it was situated at a high place in the territory of the semi-heathen Gibeonites. As hard is it to explain how ark and tabernacle came to be separated. In the wilderness the ark occupied a very subordinate position, for it appears in a list of the furniture and the vessels which were employed in the cult at the Tabernacle. Yet here it has not only become independent, but has become the centre of a cult of its own. Finally, it is at least remarkable to discover Zadok, whom Solomon made high priest in the Temple, already consecrated and officiating in a sanctuary which existed before the time of his father. To the writer who introduced this note, the cult of the ark at David's shrine in Jerusalem was not the first centre of worship in Judah. There was a sanctuary which owed its origin to the law of the Lord, in which the altar was served by a priesthood which did not owe its consecration to any king.

Again, when David consulted God about his desire to substitute for the curtains round the ark a more worthy resting-place, there appears a curious clumsiness in the prophet's reply in both versions. When he described the conditions in early Israel, the author of Samuel made the prophet state that God had never dwelt in a house, but had hitherto been walking in a tent and in a tabernacle. In I Chr. 17: 5 God is said to have replied to Nathan's inquiry that He had been from a tent to a tent and from a tabernacle.[1] Neither reading can be called satisfactory. Kittel has proposed to improve the hopeless reading in Chronicles by adding 'to a tabernacle' after 'from a tabernacle', but must add a query to his proposal, since his only authority for the addition is the Latin version. Even if the emendation were accepted, it would fail to remove the radical difficulty which is common to both passages. God is represented as having been in both a tent and a tabernacle since the day that He brought the children of Israel out of Egypt. During the wilderness journey and throughout the period of the Judges, therefore, both tent and tabernacle had been in existence, and each of them had been accounted the divine abode. The tabernacle has been introduced into the narrative, perhaps in a marginal note which has been incorporated into the text, by the same reviser who added it in chap. 16. He practically wrote—N.B. by the tent here is meant the tabernacle—for to him the temple took the place of the original tabernacle. As before, however, he failed to say what became of it during the period of the Judges.

Finally, on the occasion of the theophany at the threshing-floor of Araunah, it is stated that, when David received the divine response, he sacrificed there, 21: 28. Obviously this can only refer to the king's further use of the altar on which the fire from heaven had fallen. A site which had received so august an approval could not be deserted: this was indeed the house of the Lord and this the altar of burnt-offering

---

[1] The above is a literal version of the Hebrew, which the LXX has helped out by reading: but I was in a tent and in a tabernacle.

for Israel, 22: 1. The close connexion of these verses is broken by the statement which separates them: for the tabernacle of the Lord which Moses made in the wilderness and the altar of burnt-offering were at that time in the high place at Gibeon, but David was afraid to employ that altar because of the sword of the angel. The statement about the Araunah threshing-floor being the house of the Lord is thus made to apply to the tabernacle with its altar. But the verses, besides breaking the original connexion, contradict the terms of the theophany, since the command to the king to build the altar came directly from the angel. After his order had been obeyed, and after the divine fire had descended in approval of the sacrifice, the angel put up his sword into its sheath. We have a third addition from the same hand as in the two former cases. Again he intervened with the reminder that before an altar was built in Jerusalem Israel was possessed of a sanctuary and a cult which could claim the authority of Moses himself. Anything which David could provide for worship in the city was either subordinate, as in the case of the ark with its tent, or a mere makeshift, like the altar, due to temporary conditions. The temple took the place of the tabernacle, and its altar was the one which Bezalel made in the wilderness.[1]

When once we have recognized the leading themes of the narrator and the peculiar attitude which dominated the narrator's story of David, it is possible to trace how he dealt with his material, omitting here, supplementing there, and making the changes which he did. The other material has been added to this original narrative, and does not profess to be an independent record. It simply supplements that to which it has been added, by supplying certain caveats in the interest of another view of the course of events.

There is one other reference to the tabernacle in David's lifetime, I Chr. 23:26, but, since the verse occurs in a passage

---

[1] Kittel has already recognized v. 29 f. to be an addition. Since, however, he did not go farther and seek for the reason which had prompted such an addition, he included v. 28.

which raises other issues, it is passed over here.[1] The
sanctuary, however, appears prominently under Solomon
in the account of the young king's visit to the high place at
Gibeon and of the revelation which he received there. The
versions of this incident which appear in our two sources are
very divergent. K made the visit the first act of Solomon
after his accession, and set it in close relation to the events
which followed and preceded. He had described the palace
intrigue which had only been defeated by the influence of
Bathsheba over the old king, and had dwelt on the strength
of the opposition which Solomon needed to face. Because
the throne of the new king was by no means secure, he made
the visit to Gibeon a personal affair in order to be assured
of the divine approval and help. Accordingly, Solomon
prayed for wisdom to fulfil his new functions and minister
justice to his people, I Kings 3: 4–15. K. found it necessary
to explain why on such an occasion Solomon had recourse to
a high place, for he added that, so long as the temple was
not yet in existence, the people were still using these local
sanctuaries, and that the one point in which Solomon failed
to keep the statutes of his father was that he also frequented
them, vv. 2 f. As the historian thus linked up the revelation
at Gibeon with what preceded it, so he related it to that
which followed, for he continued with the statement that
Solomon, on his return to Jerusalem, acknowledged the
grace he had received by a public sacrifice before the ark.
Since this sacrifice included שלמים or peace-offerings, v. 15,
it was different from that at Gibeon which consisted only of
burnt-offerings, v. 4: the one was personal in its character,
the other was communal. Further, K introduced here the
story of the judgement of Solomon. Through that decision
of the new king all Israel learned to fear him, for they
recognized that the wisdom of God was in him to do judgement, v. 28. The prayer at Gibeon had been answered.

The parallel version to this is found in II Chr. 1: 1–13.
So far as the content of the prayer and of the divine message

---

[1] See pp. 71 ff.

is concerned, there is little difference between the two. The record in Chronicles is somewhat shorter than the other, and has made the message take the form of a direct revelation, instead of an appearance in a dream. It is the setting in which the incident is placed which shows the divergent point of view. The later author made Solomon's visit to Gibeon a public, instead of a private act. To him Solomon had been solemnly put forward by David as his divinely chosen successor and had been accepted by all the leaders of Israel. He, therefore, needed no confirmation of his authority. Nor was the sanctuary at Gibeon an ordinary high place, which was suspect like the similar shrines in Israel, for it contained the tabernacle which Moses the man of God made in the wilderness, and possessed the altar which Bezalel the son of Uri had made. Since it was endowed with such authority, there was no need for any explanation of the king's act in visiting it: K's introductory apology for the royal visit disappeared. In the same way the king paid no personal visit to the shrine: before he went he convened the leaders of Israel, and when he went he was attended by the קָהָל or community. The first official act of the new reign was to recognize the supreme authority of the sanctuary, which his father had been prevented from acknowledging in the day when he was afraid because of the sword of the angel of the Lord. Accordingly the king's return to the city was followed by no sacrifice before the ark and no feast to the people: the communal sacrifice had already taken place before the tabernacle. The ark received no notice in the narrative except that it was where David had placed it in its tent: and there the writer avoided the use of the word מָקוֹם or shrine, though its omission made bad Hebrew. Equally did the story of the royal judgement disappear: Solomon's authority needed no confirmation, since the nation had already acquiesced in the divine election of its new king.

This version of the incident so clearly contradicts in certain significant points the earlier account that the aim of the writer must have been to supersede the story in Kings. The only question which can arise is to determine whether it derived from the original in Chronicles, or was the work of the annotator. In my judgement it must be referred to the second hand. What he had previously suggested by a note here and another there, he now stated at length, and placed, before the description of Solomon's work on the temple, his conviction that the temple was no novelty in Israel, but had been an integral part of the national religion, since the time when Moses received the law at Horeb. Whether he substituted his version for a simpler original, or whether the whole was his own work, it is impossible to determine. Yet it ought to be acknowledged that, since the material has nothing with which it can be compared, the above conclusion is more uncertain than in the other cases, where a note can be recognized through its disturbance of the context. Its acceptance must depend on the general conclusion a student draws from the other evidence on the annotations.

When the temple was completed, Solomon summoned the leading men in Israel to bring up the ark of the covenant out of the city of David. In the presence of these men during Israel's holy week the levites, according to Chronicles, the priests, according to Kings, took up the ark. What they brought up to the temple, however, was not merely the ark, but also the tent of meeting and all the holy vessels that were in the tent.[1] The appearance of the tabernacle in this connexion is, to say the least, surprising. The men have been convened in order to bring up the ark, its porters have been appointed and have taken up their burden. The scene is at the sanctuary in David's city. But suddenly we are transported to the other sanctuary at Gibeon, where another set of porters take up the tabernacle and its sacred vessels. Are we to suppose that the assembled representatives of the nation went first to the city of David and then proceeded to Gibeon, or were there two contingents, one of which went down to the lower city and the other to the high place, after

[1] II Chr. 5: 2-5; I Kings 8: 1-4.

which, each carrying its sacred burden, they converged at the temple? To note this awkward situation brings forward another feature in the description. When Solomon convened the people for the purpose of bringing the ark into the temple, he was fulfilling the charge laid upon him by his father at the time of his accession: and, when the levites deposited the ark with the vessels that were in its tent, he and the national leaders exactly carried out the orders issued to them. Naturally they left the tent of the ark behind, since the temple had taken its place. On the other hand, when the porters brought up the tabernacle, they were acknowledging the sacredness of the sanctuary which Solomon had honoured in the first official sacrifice of his reign, but which his father was never reported to have visited.[1] He could not have ignored the sacred emblems, tabernacle and altar, which bore the great name of Moses. Again, if the sudden emergence of the tabernacle raises these difficulties, its entire disappearance remains unaccountable. For the account continues with the deposition of the ark in the temple, after which the glory of the Lord filled the house. David's purpose, when he planned the new house of God, was completed. But what place had the tabernacle in this sequence of events? It was not mentioned, when the king convened the national leaders, and nothing was said as to its ultimate destination. When C described the transference of the ark with the vessels in its tent, he ignored the tent itself, since the temple took its place. When the annotator introduced the transference of the tabernacle, he forgot that, when that which is perfect is come, then that which is in part must be done away.[2]

---

[1] To notice this connexion between the removal of the tabernacle and the royal visit, in Chronicles, thrusts into more glaring prominence how unsuitable is the mention of the tabernacle in Kings. For that book said nothing of the presence of this sanctuary in Gibeon, made Solomon's visit to the high place unofficial, and even felt it necessary to apologize for it.

[2] It is interesting to compare Bertheau's note, because it shows him

The services on the occasion served a double purpose, the חֲנֻכָּה or dedication of the temple and the celebration of the festival of Booths. The hanukkah came first, I Kings 8: 63, II Chr. 7: 5. As for the festival, there are two interesting points of divergence between the records in I Kings 8: 64–6 and II Chr. 7: 7–10. The earlier writer called the altar, which was found too small for the sacrifices at the festival, simply the altar which was before the Lord: the later called it the altar which Solomon had made, and, when he referred to the hanukkah, named that the dedication of the altar, not of the temple. Again, the writer in Kings made the celebration of the festival last only a week, for in his account the worshippers returned to their homes on the eighth day. He may even have made the two ceremonies run con-currently and together last no more than a week, for the clause at the close of his v. 65, according to which they lasted fourteen days, is absent from the LXX. In Chronicles, on the other hand, an additional day or עֲצֶרֶת was added to the festival, and so the use of Jerusalem at Booths was made to conform from the beginning with the practice prescribed in the later law, Lev. 23: 36; Num. 29: 35.

When, however, we turn to the description of the dedi-cation service in Chronicles, the situation is much more perplexing and involved. Thus there are two series of sacri-fices at 5: 6 and at 7: 1. One of these preceded, the other followed Solomon's prayer. Twice also the glory of the Lord is said to have filled the temple, so that the priests were unable to continue their duties in it, 5: 14, 7: 1f. In the latter case it is added that fire descended from heaven and consumed the offerings. Kittel is of opinion that the sacrifice which followed Solomon's prayer was a personal offering

to have had a suspicion of the real situation. There is a minor, but not wholly negligible, difficulty in the phrase, 'the ark and the tent of meeting and the holy vessels that were in the tent'. According to the law in Numbers the ark was one of those holy vessels of the tabernacle. Yet here it has not only escaped from that subordinate position, but is mentioned first.

on the part of the king, which in turn was succeeded by the offerings of king and people in v. 4. This is an impossible interpretation, for the sacrifice which followed the royal prayer was attended both by the descent of the divine fire and the appearance of the divine glory. Now the descent of the fire from heaven was meant to imply that the sacrifice which it consumed was accepted and the altar on which it came down was legitimate. The theophany which filled the temple implied that the dedication was complete. The connexion between the two acts of sacrifice here is that for a time the altar, which had received its consecration, was inaccessible to the priests because of the divine glory. As soon, however, as this had abated, the altar was employed for the celebration of the festival of Booths. The altar which was thus consecrated was the one which Solomon had made, v. 7, and so significant was its consecration that the writer here called the whole ceremony the dedication of the altar, v. 9.

The course of events after Solomon's prayer appears straightforward enough. The real difficulty is to reconcile this with the events which preceded the prayer, for there we read of a similar public and communal sacrifice, which was followed by the descent of the cloud to indicate that the dedication of the temple was complete. The sacrifices in this case were offered before the ark, which is prominent here, but of which nothing is said after the prayer: on the other hand, there is no mention of the descent of the divine fire, nor of an altar Solomon made, on which the fire fell. How prominent a position was given to the ark appears from four features of the earlier account. As soon as it was deposited in the Temple, sacrifices were offered before it. It is added that there it remains to this day, 5:9c.[1] When the

---

[1] There is no need to alter the MT here, which reads ויהי, in order to bring it into agreement with the plural reading in Kings. This change, commonly accepted though it is, fails to explain the peculiar reading in Chronicles, and makes the sentence pointless. What, according to the new text, is said to remain to this day is the protruding staves of the

sacrifices before the ark were consumed, the glory of the
Lord filled the Temple and completed the hanukkah. When
this was over, and the ceremony had thus come to its end,
Solomon rose, not to offer prayer, but to declare what had
been done. In his statement he reverted to the charge he
had received in the presence of the people on the day of his
accession, and declared that he had not failed to fulfil it.
I am risen up in the room of David my father, and sit on the
throne of Israel, as the Lord promised, and have built the
house for the name of the Lord, the God of Israel, and there
have I set the ark, wherein is the covenant of the Lord,
6: 10 f.

This reconstructed account of the hanukkah reproduces
the features which characterized the work of C. The temple
was a surrogate for the tent of the ark.

When, therefore, the temple was complete, the ark was
brought into it. On its arrival at its final resting-place
sacrifices were offered before it. Thereupon, in token that
everything necessary for the dedication of the new sanctuary
had been completed, the glory of the Lord filled the house,
in which the ark remained to this day: and Solomon was able
to declare in the presence of the assembled people that the
task his father had committed to him had been fulfilled. It
was not necessary that Solomon should build an altar for the
sacrifices or for the heavenly fire to declare it acceptable.
The altar, on which the sacrifices before the ark were offered,
had been erected long before by David on the Araunah
threshing-floor. It had then received its consecration by the
descent of the fire from heaven, and David, in recognition
of the theophany, had declared this to be the house of the
Lord God and the altar of burnt-offering for Israel.

The other account, which follows Solomon's prayer,
equally bears the sign-manual of the annotator. To him
the centre of interest was the tabernacle with its altar.

ark, but one cannot fail to wonder why these should be of such lively
interest to any one. The original singular was altered in Kings into
a plural, after the preceding verses had been added.

Therefore he made Solomon bring up the tabernacle, for the temple was built to take its place. Because he had made David's altar at the time of the pestilence into a mere make-shift, due to the king's inability to reach Gibeon with its altar, Solomon must construct a new altar, on which, since it required the divine approval, the fire from heaven descended. So essential was this to the efficacy of the sacrifices which were to be offered there that he could call the whole ceremony the dedication of the altar. His account dovetails into his previous notes, as C's account dovetails into his earlier material.

But the annotator was not content to supply a parallel version of the dedication of the temple.[1] He inserted at least two paragraphs into C's narrative, the purpose of which it is possible to recognize. After the levites had brought the ark into the temple and after the sacrifices before it, he made the priests carry it into the holy of holies and deposit it there. In that inner shrine it disappeared from the sight of the worshippers, so that no more sacrifices could be offered before it. After that, he could continue with C's conclusion—and there it remains to this day, since now the sentence meant that the emblem was relegated to the background. There was no need for it to be prominent in connexion with the cult, since it was nothing but a receptacle for the stone tablets which formed the memorial of the divine covenant with Israel.[2] Again, when the priests returned from the inner sanctuary, the ceremony continued. But only the priests were permitted to surround the altar: the levites, who had carried up the ark and who had been its ministers in its tent, were not now allowed to advance beyond the

[1] The same method is followed in the account of Hezekiah's reform. There are two versions of his hanukkah, cf. pp. 105 ff.

[2] For another mention of this employment of the ark, and for the evidence that it implied a quiet degradation of the emblem from its original position, cf. my *Deuteronomy, the Framework to the Code*, p. 64 f. For a similar proof of the desire to dismiss the ark into the background cf. my *Post-Exilic Judaism*, p. 230 f.

east end of the altar. At that careful distance they were
entrusted with the musical accompaniment of the rite,
though the use of the trumpets was committed to the priests.[1]
After the ark had been thus consigned to its fitting resting-
place in the hidden shrine, and after the officiating clergy
had been arranged with due regard to their ecclesiastical
dignity, the glory of the Lord filled the house. The theophany was removed from its dangerously suggestive neigh-
bourhood to the sacrifices before the ark.

In all this the annotator showed his knowledge of the later
law and a scrupulous regard for its observance. When the
priests carried the ark into the inner sanctuary, they were
acting according to the law in Num. 4: 5 ff. When an extra
day was added to the week of the festival of Booths, the
regulations for the festal occasions in Num. cc. 28 f. were
observed. The procedure followed after Solomon's prayer
closely resembled that which attended the completion of the
tabernacle in Lev. 9: 22–4. There Moses and Aaron came
out to the front of the tabernacle and blessed the people.
Thereupon the glory of the Lord appeared to the congregation, the fire from heaven consumed the offerings, and the
people prostrated themselves. In the temple they prostrated
themselves on the רִצְפָּה or pavement, an expression which
is peculiar to this passage and to Ezek. 42: 3, 40: 17 f.

---

[1] Kittel pronounced 5: 11b to 13a to be an addition, but he saw in it
a desire to assert the dignity of the levites by giving them a due share in
the ceremonial through their connexion with the musical service. He
failed, however, to recognize the context in which these singers
appeared. On the one side was the statement that the levites were not
permitted to advance beyond the east side of the altar: on the other,
the trumpets were reserved to the priests, so that the levites had not
full control even over the musical service. The musical service is here a
sign of the lower status of the levitical order and is contrasted with the
function of the priests who alone officiated at the altar.

II

THE CHRONICLER AND PROPHECY

A FEATURE in the Chronicler's narrative is the prominent position he gave to prophecy in relation to the kingdom. When all Israel came to Hebron and elected David to be their king, they were fulfilling the divine purpose, for their act was according to the word of God through Samuel. Prophecy did more than accept the kingdom, it had been a controlling factor in its foundation; the new institution owed its existence to the will of God revealed through His servants. Similarly, when Jerusalem fell before Nebuchadrezzar, the catastrophe was not wholly due to Zedekiah's breach of his oath of fealty to his suzerain, but was also due to the king's failure to humble himself before Jeremiah the prophet from the mouth of the Lord, II. 36: 12. The neglect of prophecy had been a leading factor in the overthrow of the kingdom which it had helped to found.

These are the two foci round which all C's thoughts about the kingdom in Israel turned. But he did not leave the two judgements isolated, one at the beginning, the other at the end, of his story. He linked them together by a thread which runs through his record of the successive kings. When David received the promise that God meant to make him the first of a dynasty, he also received the reminder that the promise was conditional. The kingdom in Israel depended on the faithfulness of his successors in keeping the divine law and obeying the divine word. The needed divine direction was to be found by them, not merely in the precepts of the law: it was continually revealed through the living voice of prophecy. For C introduced into his narrative a series of prophets who appeared before the successive kings in order to warn them of the policy they ought to follow or to rebuke them for their failure in fulfilling the divine will. How fundamental these stories were to C's thoughts about the kingdom is clear from the fact that they are all peculiar to his account. Only in one instance did he borrow a prophetic message from his predecessor, when he reproduced almost verbatim the appearance of Micaiah ben Imlah before Jehoshaphat and Ahab at the opening of the campaign against Ramoth Gilead. The chief interest in the one prophetic story which he copied is to be found, as will appear later, in the contrast between its inimitable power and the accounts which derive from his own pen. According to the Chronicler, prophecy, which made the kingdom possible and condemned it in the end, accompanied the institution throughout its course.

The first case occurs at the time of Shishak's invasion of Palestine during the reign of Rehoboam.[1] Here C introduced a prophet Shemaiah who pronounced the invasion to be the divine penalty for the sin of the nation in that it had forsaken its God. When the people repented, the prophet declared that the calamity would not result in their ruin, though it must bring a severe chastisement for their transgression. The divine anger was averted because of this repentance and because some good things were found in Israel; but the kingdom was maintained when king and people obeyed the warning voice of the prophet.

In the reign of Asa Zerah the Ethiopian advanced against Judah with an overwhelming army. The king betook himself to prayer and closed with the petition: We rely on Thee and in Thy name are we come against this multitude. O Lord, Thou art our God; let not man prevail against Thee. The result was that God Himself smote the Ethiopians, leaving to Asa and his army no other task than that of pursuing the broken army, II. 14: 9–14. Thereupon a prophet Azariah ben Oded met the returning conquerors and drove home the appropriate lesson, 15: 1–7. He fortified his sermon by appealing in somewhat puzzling terms to the past experience of the nation, but his main theme was to stress the devotion of the king to the divine will and to

[1] II Chr. c. 12, cf. I Kings 14: 21–31.

encourage him to maintain a similar attitude by the assurance that such conduct could never fail to receive its reward. Apparently the prophet approved in Asa more than his absolute dependence on the divine help, for it is said that the king had already removed the foreign altars and high places, had broken the mazzeboth and cut down the asherim, and had commanded Judah to keep the law and the commandment, 14: 2 f. The prophecy was intended to encourage him to proceed in the same direction, 15: 8. When, however, Asa was attacked by Baasha of Israel, he took a different course, for he bribed the king of Damascus to come to his help. At once Hanani the seer denounced his policy along the same lines as had led Azariah to commend his previous conduct, and declared that the result must be continuous war. The king's act in appealing to Syria was condemned, not because he had allied himself with a heathen power, but because he had sought human help at all. He ought to have trusted his kingdom to the divine support, 16: 1–9.[1]

When Jehoshaphat returned from the disastrous campaign against Ramoth Gilead, Jehu ben Hanani met him and declared that the catastrophe was due to the divine anger because of the help which he had given to the wicked Ahab.

[1] In the interests of his theory C here departed entirely from the chronology of Kings. While he followed K somewhat closely in the account of the campaign between Judah and Israel, he made the Israelite attack Judah in the 36th year of Asa: K, on the other hand, made the war between the kings last all their days. Besides, the 36th year of Asa as the date for the outbreak of the war hopelessly conflicts with K's statement that Baasha died in the 26th year of Asa. The usual explanation of the discrepancy is to suppose that here C was following a different source. In my judgement it is more simply accounted for on the view that C adapted his chronology in order to suit his theory. The great deliverance from Zerah, which he alone reported, and which it is very difficult to accept as literal history, must have been followed by a period of peace which was the reward for Asa's trust in God, just as the continuous war and the king's disease in his feet resulted from his faithlessness. Room must be found, even at the cost of upsetting the chronology, for these successive events.

Yet the seer modified the condemnation, because some good elements remained in the king and because he had abolished the asheroth and set his heart to seek the Lord. After this warning Jehoshaphat continued his work of reform by improving the administration of justice, chap. 19. He further proved how well he had taken to heart the lesson he had received, for, when an overwhelming host of enemies from the East invaded Judah, he followed the example of Asa and betook himself to fasting and prayer, chap. 20. Thereupon the divine spirit came upon a levite Yahaziel who promised a complete deliverance from the danger. The faith of the king and the promise of the prophet were justified, for on the following day the invaders were routed without Judah being required to strike a blow.

Again, when Amaziah had gathered an army against the children of Seir, he judged them insufficient for the task and hired a body of troops from Israel. But an unnamed prophet intervened and bade the king recognize that no success could attend him, if he employed men with whom the Lord could have nothing to do, 25: 6–12. Unfortunately, the text of v. 8 is uncertain so that it is impossible to decide whether the prophet's objection was principally directed against the employment of Israelite mercenaries, or whether such tainted support merely aggravated the king's sin in failing to rely on the sufficient help of God. The issue of the campaign may at least justify the latter conclusion, for, while Amaziah won a brilliant victory after he had dismissed the Israelite troops, the disappointed mercenaries fell upon and looted a number of towns in Judah. The author may have wished to point out that, though the king's obedience to the prophetic warning brought his army success, his initial fault in employing men from Samaria did not fail to bring down a merited penalty. After his victory Amaziah took home with him the gods of the conquered people and worshipped them. The act brought a strong protest from another unnamed prophet, but this time the offender, instead of listening to the rebuke, insulted the divine messenger with the result that he received the promise of his ruin, vv.13–16. The incident forms in Chronicles the introduction to the disastrous war against Israel.

This series of incidents is not exactly parallel to another series which might be collated, in which a king's defeat was traced to his failure to maintain loyal adherence to the national religion. Outwardly, the special features in the events which have been brought together are that they are all peculiar to the Chronicler and that they are all attended by the appearance of a prophet. But inwardly they are also peculiar in that they introduce a novel standard for the conduct of the kings and of their court. K's customary judgement on the successive kings was based on whether they maintained strict loyalty to Yahwism, with a special attention to whether they observed the law of the single sanctuary. C did not fail to recognize that standard, though it deserves to be noted that he did not always reproduce the strictures of K about the abolition or non-abolition of the high places. But it is significant to discover that he extended the principle of absolute allegiance to Yahweh, and made it cover more than loyalty to the national cult and the law. In everything which concerned the maintenance of his kingdom, a king of Judah must be wholly dependent on the divine help. Even to rely too much on the nation's own strength was to show insufficient trust in God; and to enter into alliance with a foreign power, even if that power were the sister-nation, was to forfeit the divine support. The kingdom which owed its origin to the divine intervention needed no more for its continuance. To seek other help was to question the divine sufficiency to maintain what God had brought into being. When, therefore, C introduced into his narrative the series of prophets who all enforced the same principle, he acknowledged the source from which he derived the new standard which he applied to the kingdom and to its kings. It did not come from the law of Israel, but in his judgement it had formed the burden of prophecy. To him this dogma represented the leading conviction of the prophets in relation to the kingdom, and he did not hesitate to make the course of the history of the kingdom and the fate which befell the successive kings conform to it. The words which he put into the mouth of Jehoshaphat were the epitome of his attitude on the subject: believe in the Lord your God, so shall ye be established, believe His prophets, so shall ye prosper, 20: 20. Since the earlier half of the saying is the positive form of an oracle which appears in its negative form at Isa. 7: 9, it is evident that he believed himself to be reproducing the prophetic attitude on the question. If he misinterpreted the Isaianic message, it must be added that he did so in numerous company. His view was that of the court prophets who urged Zedekiah into rebellion, because Yahweh must protect His city and the temple within it; and it is still that of all the moderns who believe that Isaiah taught the inviolability of Jerusalem, because its temple was the place which Yahweh had chosen for His abode, and who believe that the prophet saw in the temporary defeat of Assyria the vindication of his dogma.

The series of prophets, however, all of whom rebuke or hearten the kings of Israel, throws light on the Chronicler's idea of the kingdom as well as on his idea of the burden of prophecy. It brings sharply into view how strictly in his judgement the continuance of the kingdom was conditioned by the policy of the royal court. There are expressions employed in the promise of God to raise up and maintain a Davidic dynasty which have led several careful students to believe that a certain Messianic dignity was attached to the house of David. We are not concerned with the general question here, but merely with the particular question as to whether the Chronicler shared that opinion. Von Rad collated the evidence on the subject,[1] and pointed out that the promise to the Davidic king was always conditional on the loyalty of the successive kings to the divine commandments. Writing after Von Rad and recognizing his careful sifting of the relative passages, I agreed with his conclusions

[1] In his *Geschichtsbild des chronistischen Werkes*.

and stated that the figure of the Davidic king never escaped from the limits of time or even from those of human frailty; he, like all his subjects, was under the torah.[1] But neither of us realized the force of this series of prophetic utterances, which prove that to the Chronicler prophecy had always attended the kingdom, and that one of its leading functions had been to guide the kings in the only policy which could guarantee to them the divine protection and support. The Davidic kings were not merely, like all their subjects, under the torah: they were also controlled by the authentic voice of God, uttered by the prophets. Only if they obeyed that voice, could they expect the divine furtherance. Whenever one of the royal line ignored the divine counsel he brought his kingdom into danger, and even to the verge of ruin. Whenever he repented of his disobedience he received the deliverance which only God could bring him in his straits. When, on the other hand, he followed the counsel of the prophet, no enemy, however overwhelming his host might be, had been able to prevail against Israel. The intervention of God had been of such a character in these circumstances that it was impossible to mistake its source, for Israel had required to do nothing but stand still and see the deliverance which God wrought. The continuance of the kingdom had been always conditioned on the obedience of the kings to the word of prophecy which had brought the kingdom into existence. The condition was so absolute in its character that when the last king, ignoring the lessons of the past, despised the message of a prophet, his kingdom fell.

The important place which the Chronicler thus gave to prophecy in the national life makes it natural to ask how he conceived of the institution in itself. He retained a sense of the charismatic character which had belonged to it. For on one occasion he told how the Spirit of the Lord came upon a levite, who did not belong to the court circle, and on another he related that the Lord sent a prophet to Amaziah, from whom the king scornfully demanded whether he had

[2] *Post-Exilic Judaism*, pp. 192 ff.

ever been appointed to the royal council. He thus retained from the past the independent character of the prophetic message. Throughout all the stories the successive prophets had no hesitation in reproving the royal conduct and, when they supported it, the support was given to actions which conformed with their own teaching. The men were no mere courtiers, lending the support of their authority to the royal policy. In general, however, he thought of the prophets as having a recognized position about the court. When he referred to their writings, as he very frequently did, he had no hesitation in calling them the king's seers. He could even ascribe to David the institution of a guild of levites, all of whose leaders were called seers or prophets, and whose function was to prophesy to the accompaniment of music, I. 25: 1 f. Men could be trained to carry on this most individual function.

What shows the wide departure from the older position is to recognize the character of the message which the men brought. It has become stereotyped, for all the successive prophets really say the same thing. There is a lack of individuality about their words, and one cannot escape from the sense that each of them was repeating what it was the recognized thing for a prophet to say. The Chronicler was following a tradition which he did not vary, except in its terms. The older prophets followed tradition, but that took the form of certain great convictions which the men applied to the conditions and circumstances of their own time. There was room for individuality of outlook and judgement, not merely for variation of language. Now the men conform to a pattern, and almost subscribe to a dogma. When C quoted in its entirety from K the encounter between Ahab and Micaiah ben Imlah he showed himself sensitive to the power of the older prophecy, but unconsciously he invited comparison between that vivid story and his own tame accounts. In contrast with the tremendous figures of Elijah and Amos and Hosea C's prophets are colourless and thin, and have become mouthpieces of a recognized message.

H

The historian belonged to a time when prophecy was on its death-bed, as an active force in the life of the nation. Men could still read and admire the great messages which had come down from the past, but they were no longer able to prophesy. Israel had passed from the period of creation with its ferment and its place for personal conviction, and had reached the period of the makers of systems, the theologians and the ecclesiastics. The institution had arrived and was busy with its customary task of canalizing the fruitful and dangerous religious tides in the national life.

But the spirit of the past was not yet dead. Though men could not prophesy themselves, they remained conscious of the value of one of the peculiar and most powerful factors in their national life. A man who could not write the story of his nation without a constant reference to prophecy and its work was alive to its worth. It had contributed an invaluable element to that kingdom which was now a mere memory. The kingdom of Israel had not been a shortlived example of the many which appeared in the ever-changing pattern of its world. What was distinctive in it had not been entirely derived from the temple and its cult which still survived: it had in part been due to the succession of men who had borne constant and fearless witness to standards of life which, because they were eternal, ought to influence so mutable a thing as a royal policy.

A further evidence of the value which the Chronicler attached to prophecy is to be found in the extent to which he referred his readers to sources of that character in the conclusions he appended to the life of each of the kings. For David he cited the words of Samuel the seer, of Nathan the prophet, and of Gad the seer, I. 29: 29; and for Solomon the words of Nathan the prophet, the prophecy of Ahijah the Shilonite, and the visions of Iddo the seer, II. 9: 29. The acts of Rehoboam were written in the words of Shemaiah the prophet and of Iddo the seer II. 12: 15; the rest of the acts, ways, and sayings of Abijah in the midrash of Iddo the prophet, II. 13: 22. The rest of the acts of Jehoshaphat were to be found in the words of Jehu ben Hanani which are inserted (or who is mentioned) in the book of the Kings of Israel, II. 20: 34. Information concerning the sons of Joash and the greatness of the burdens upon or against him, and concerning his restoration of the temple is to be found in the midrash of the book of the Kings, II. 24: 27. The rest of the acts of Uzziah did Isaiah ben Amoz the prophet write, II. 26: 22; the rest of the acts of Hezekiah and his good deeds were written in the vision of Isaiah ben Amoz the prophet in the book of the Kings of Judah and Israel, II. 32: 32. The rest of the acts of Manasse and his prayer and the words of the seers who spoke to him in the name of the Lord were preserved among the acts of the Kings of Israel: his prayer also and all his sin and trespass before he humbled himself were written in the history of Hozai, for which the LXX reads the seers, II. 33: 18 f.

The list contains only the references which are peculiar to C; a complete list would require the inclusion of those which are common to him and K. It is also a feature of his account that his appeals to supplementary sources of this character are more frequent in the earlier period of the kingdom, and that after Hezekiah and Manasse they disappear.

Another feature of the series of oracles and the incidents in which they are imbedded is that there is no evidence of their having received any serious attention from the reviser; any notes added to them are negligible.

It is clear, then, both from the extent to which he referred to the works of the prophets and from the oracles which he inserted in his own narrative, that the Chronicler felt himself in sympathy with, or even wished to be regarded as continuing this type of literature. And it is possible to recognize already how far his work departed, not merely from our modern method of writing history, but from the method in which the authors of Samuel and Kings wrote it. With the means at their disposal these men did place David in the stream of the national life, and show to some extent how the past had made his life-work possible, and how the same past set limits on what he could do. They never hid the fact of the radical division in the nation, which his personality had overcome, but only with difficulty and only for a time. In the same way they made him the founder of a dynasty, but confessed that even his immediate successor only reached the throne through a harem-intrigue. The Chronicler did not see the figure of David in the light of history: he saw him, as it were, *sub specie aeternitatis*, which meant to the Hebrew that he saw the king to have been the instrument of the divine purpose in Israel. David was designated by a prophet for the throne before he reached it, and he was elected by the whole nation, when God had intervened to blot out the house of Saul. His dynasty had endured, not because the successive kings had been able to make good their claim to the throne, but because God had promised to build him a house. The kingdom as well as its founder was an instrument by which God purposed to work out His will for His chosen people. Because it was such an instrument, it could rely on His support, for He would intervene to protect it against all its enemies. In order that it might realize its function in the world, God had sent a succession of prophets, through whom the successive kings were reminded that they were chosen to serve a greater will than their own. When the men listened and obeyed, when they acknowledged that the protection of their God was sufficient for Israel, He had intervened and had made good His promise. But when the dynasty refused to listen, and when its last king turned his back on the divine warning, the kingdom came to its end. It had failed to fulfil the purpose which its God had in mind when He brought it into being.

Yet that was not and could not be the end, for there could be no end to the purpose of God with His nation. So the Chronicler wove into the history of the kingdom the history of the temple and supplemented the account of his predecessor by this record. The first king, himself divinely elected, planned the sanctuary for his people. He laid down the lines along which its building was to be carried out, and determined the functions of the ministers who were to conduct its worship: he even chose its site. In every stage of his growing scheme and in every part of the plans he formed he was guided by revelation. After every desecration of the sacred building came a reforming king who restored the conditions which had been designed by its founder, for these had been invested from the first with divine authority. The kingdom, as an institution, had failed; but it did not disappear, until it had brought into existence an institution which outlasted itself. The Davidic dynasty had been disloyal to the conditions on which alone it could expect to be continued. But through its best representatives the house of David had built up something which could endure to be the centre for Israel's life.

The author of Kings had written the history of the time when Israel had taken its place among the nations of the world. Under David Judah and Samaria and Transjordan had been blended into a unity which gave them strength to assert their independence, and even to conquer some of the surrounding nations. He had collated the records of the past and attempted to trace the varying fortunes which had attended the successive kings. Yet the story which he had to tell was in the end the record of a failure, and could at best remind his people of the greater past which had once been theirs, though now it had disappeared. It could not give them anything which was fitted to help them in their dolorous present or to enable them to face the future.

The Chronicler believed in the future, because he believed that his people was elect after the counsel of God. To him the kingdom was but one stage in the long road down which its God was leading Israel. Therefore, although the institution had collapsed and could never return, it had sheltered the germ which could maintain the nation's life. He added to what his predecessor had told the story of the temple, dwelling on how the first king planned it with loving care, and how his true successors did not fail to restore it to its true place in the national life. For he was writing to and for a generation which had recovered from the disaster of the Exile and had begun to plan a polity which made the cult the centre for Jewry. Convinced himself that this was the hope of Israel, he sought to convince his fellow Jews of the thing in which he believed. He was not writing history; he was writing a tract for his times, in which he used history, in order to enforce his convictions. He was attempting to extract from the past the lessons which it could supply in order to guide the future. The end at which he aimed affected even his style. Compared with Kings, his review of the history of the kingdom can only be called flat and dull. All the picturesque elements in the record, stories like those of David's flight from Jerusalem, or the meeting of Micaiah ben Imlah with Ahab, or the account of the plague in David's day, with their vivid lights on men's character and their power to show the past in its concrete reality, have either been borrowed or omitted by him. His material was forced to submit to the end which he had in view. Every man who is engrossed in his own task produces work which is tame and dull to a later generation. The sermons and pamphlets which were written to serve one time are apt to appear unreadable when that time is past. They demand that men put themselves back to a distant point of view, before later men can even begin to measure and appreciate their influence.

The Chronicler was not writing history: he was attempting in his own way to determine what men might gather from the review of their past as to the ways of God with the Israel which He had made His own. If we define *midrash* as an interpretation of history, the use of the past to discover its meaning in order to illuminate and guide the present, then *midrash* was no sporadic element which crops out here and there in his treatment of his theme, but was of the essence of his work. His method also was no novelty in the life and literature of Israel, for the men who wrote the patriarchal narratives had already used it.

III

THE CHRONICLER AND THE LEVITES

AN outstanding difference between the two accounts of the kingdom in Israel is the neglect of the levites by the earlier historian contrasted with the interest which the later writer showed in those officials. Whenever the earlier books referred to the cult, they spoke of its ministers as priests. Whenever the later book introduced the officials at the temple, it spoke of them as priests and levites: sometimes it even confined its attention to the levites and made no reference to the priests. So marked is this feature in C that it is no exaggeration to say that his interest in the levitical order is a characteristic of his history. This interest appears most prominently in his account of David's plans for the temple, of Solomon's erection of the building, and of the work of the reforming kings who restored the sanctuary and its cult. One evidence of the zeal for true religion on the part of these reformers was their care for the position of this body of the clergy.

Yet C never has anything to say about the origin of the men in whom he was so deeply interested. He took them and their position in the nation for granted in the same way as his predecessor took the priests and their functions for granted. He has, however, made two general statements about them which are of interest. The men were not only recognized as a class before David planned the temple, but they possessed a peculiar dignity in connexion with the cult. C made David explain the early failure in the transference of the ark by the fact that he had not entrusted the sacred emblem into their hands. They alone were capable of handling and carrying it; and this duty was a privilege, not a sign of inferior status like their task of carrying the tabernacle and its vessels according to the law in Numbers. To infringe their privilege was enough to defeat the earlier attempt with the ark, and the success which attended the second effort vindicated their claim, and led David to frame a regulation on the subject.

The other general statement about the levites occurs in II Chr. 11 : 13 ff. In his description of the apostasy of the northern kingdom under Jeroboam, C stated, as one result of the introduction of the calf-worship, that the levites in Israel forsook the polluted territory, even at some sacrifice to themselves, and took refuge in the purer south. This implies, not only that there were levites in Israel, but that the men fulfilled certain religious functions there. The author did not define exactly what these functions were. But he thought of them as being sacrificial in character, for he stated that Jeroboam and his sons drove the men out from executing the priest's office unto the Lord. Whatever the ' suburbs ' which they sacrificed because of their loyalty may have been, these belonged to them in virtue of their office. According to C, therefore, levites existed in Israel before the temple existed, and fulfilled there priestly duties which were independent of the temple or the ark.

A. The Levites as Singers

Before entering on the general question of C's attitude to the levites, it may clear the air to examine a special matter which is related to it. The books of Chronicles contain a number of references to the musical side of the cult, and also refer to levites as those who were charged with the sacred song and its musical accompaniment. Because of this, and because of the comparative neglect of the subject in the books of Kings, it has become customary to conclude that the historian regarded this function as the peculiar duty and privilege of the entire levitical body, and it has been suggested that he may have been a member of one of the temple choirs. A scholar who has recently devoted attention to the matter finds himself able to write: 'One interest permeates the entire literature of the Chronicler, from the introduction in the first book of Chronicles down to the final chapters of the book of Nehemiah. That is the interest in the function of the levites as singers and porters. This interest is the specific interest which the Chronicler has in the levites.'[1] Vogelstein went further, for he found in this dominant feature of the book the motive which led to its composition. In his view the levites after the Return were relegated to merely menial duties about the temple, and the Chronicler's book represents an effort on the part of the levites to win a higher status through insisting on their functions as leaders of the sacred music.[2]

It may, then, be useful to collate the passages which refer to the musical service, to examine the relation of the levites to this part of the cult, and to test how far the facts justify either conclusion.

There are 24 allusions to the sacred music in that part of the books of Chronicles which is the subject of this study, if we include its use in war as well as in the temple-cult. Since war in old Israel was set under the divine direction, one may not wholly ignore the two military examples. They are as follows. When Abijah met the army of Israel, he told their king that, among its other advantages, Judah possessed the priests sounding the trumpets of alarm, and accordingly at the ensuing battle the priests sounded those trumpets, II. 13 : 12–14. On the other hand, when Moab and Ammon came up against Jehoshaphat and were destroyed through divine intervention, the levites, on the morning of Judah's bloodless triumph, stood up to praise the Lord with a loud voice, II. 20: 19. Since these references to sacred music in connexion with war give an equal position to the priests and levites, they throw no light on our question.

The other instances occur in closer association with the cult. In five of these cases the language is quite general. When the ark was being brought up to Jerusalem, David and all Israel played before God with songs, harps, psalteries,

[1] Hänel: 'Das Recht der Opferschlachtung in der chronistischen Literatur', ZAW 1937, p. 64.
[2] Der Kampf zwischen Priestern und Leviten.

timbrels, cymbals, and trumpets, I. 13 : 8. When it arrived, all Israel brought it with shouting, with cornets, trumpets, cymbals, psalteries, and harps, I. 15 : 28. On the occasion of Asa's covenant the people sware unto the Lord with shouting and with trumpets and cornets, II. 15 : 14. After their deliverance from the threat of invasion by Moab and Ammon in the reign of Jehoshaphat the people came into the temple with psalteries, harps, and trumpets, II. 20 : 28. When Athaliah found young Joash in the temple, all the people were rejoicing and blew with trumpets, the singers also played on instruments of music, II. 23 : 13.[1] These passages throw no direct light on our question, for they contain no reference to the levites. They do, however, throw indirect light, since, even if it be supposed that the music was supplied by choirs, the fact remains that the historian did not use so excellent an opportunity for emphasizing that the choirs were composed of levites. If the connexion of the levites with the sacred music had been his ' specific interest', he would scarcely have failed to underline their part here.

There remain seventeen passages where the levites were definitely associated with the musical side of the cult. These may be divided into two classes. In the first class fall the cases where the singers and musicians were separated from the rest of their brethren, and constituted into a guild apart. Generally, the names of their leaders are given with or without the descent these men could claim from Levi. In one instance, only their numbers appear, but these are given relatively to the number of the larger body, so that again they constitute a guild apart. Thus, when the ark was transferred from the house of Obed Edom, David directed the chief of the levites to appoint their brethren the singers with musical instruments. The men so appointed were Heman, Asaph, and Ethan, I. 15 : 16–24. After its arrival in the city the

---

[1] Only the last of these citations has any parallel in K: C quoted the first part of the triumph over the coronation of Joash from II Kings 11: 14.

king commissioned certain levites to minister before the ark and to celebrate and to give praise. Accordingly Asaph and his brethren, part of the singers who had been chosen by the chiefs, appear with their musical instruments, I. 16: 1–6. Since, however, the service before the ark was not purely choral, there were other levites who had carried the emblem, a body who served before it, and a group who acted as doorkeepers.[1] Again, at v. 7 David ordained to give thanks by Asaph and his brethren, and at vv. 37 ff. Asaph, Heman, and Jeduthun appear in that capacity.[2] Among the arrangements made by David for the future temple, there is mention of 4,000 levites who had the duty of offering praise with musical instruments, I. 23: 5. Nothing more is said about these men, but evidently they composed a small proportion of the whole body, which is said to have been composed of 34,000 individuals. These numbers may be exaggerated; but that does not affect the proportion between 4,000 singers and 30,000 other levites who were engaged in different duties. Among the temple personnel whose functions were determined at the same time appear certain of the sons of Asaph, Heman, and Jeduthun, whom David set apart to prophesy with a musical accompaniment, I. 25: 1 ff. Their number, along with that of their brethren, only amounted to 288, v. 7. At the celebration of the passover under Josiah the singers, the sons of Asaph, were in their places according to the commandment of David, II. 35: 15, but the majority of the levites were in charge of the arrangements for the ceremony.

This final instance deserves special notice. Two bodies of levites appear: the one consisted of the larger number

[1] The fact that David was said to have decided on the 'certain levites' who served before the ark and who offered praise before it, though the singers had been already appointed to their task, is another indication that the service at the new shrine was not merely choral.

[2] The section is extremely confused and gives evidence of conflate readings, but, though it is impossible to disentangle the original with any confidence, the above conclusion remains unaffected.

who were appointed by the king to fulfil certain functions
at the passover, the other is said to have been sons of Asaph
who were entrusted with the musical service. The larger
body were ordered to prepare the paschal victims for their
brethren, the singers, who were so much engaged in their
other duties that they could not do this for themselves.
Kittel regarded the verse as an addition on the ground that
it showed the Chronicler's bias in favour of the levitical
singers. But this is to miss the real content of the remark.
What the Chronicler was interested in was that the choral
service was not intromitted, because the singers must
prepare their paschal victims like every other householder.
Its continuance was made possible, because the other
levites undertook that duty for their brethren. Instead of
regarding the levites as such to be singers, the verse makes
a clear distinction between those who were singers and the
larger number who were busy with other tasks.

There next fall to be considered the cases where we hear
nothing of a guild of singers, but merely of levites or the
levites conducting the musical service. They occur in the
story of Solomon's dedication of the temple, II. 5: 11 ff., 7: 6,
and among David's final charges, I. 23: 30; and they deserve
special consideration, because of two features which they
possess in common. On the one hand, they do not belong
to the original C, but have been intruded into his narrative.[1]
On the other hand, they all occur in passages where the
inferior status of the levites in relation to the priests was
being insisted on by the annotator. At the dedication of the
temple C made the levites carry in the ark and sacrifice
before it. The annotator made the priests take it up and
deposit it in the most holy place out of sight, and went on
to add that the levitical singers were not permitted to
advance beyond the east end of the altar. In both cases he
was relegating the inferior clergy to their fitting place and
to their lower functions. Similarly at II. 7: 6, the priests
offered the sacrifices, while the attendant levites accom-

[1] For the proof see pp. 37 ff. and p. 85.

panied them with music. At I. 23: 27 ff. the relative status of priests and levites was defined by David, and there the office of the levites was to wait upon the sons of Aaron for the service of the house of the Lord in the courts and in the chambers. Their task as musicians was merely one among the inferior duties which fell to their lot in this lower office. To stand every morning to thank and praise the Lord, and likewise every even is merely one among the miscellaneous services which the men rendered to their superiors. In the same way, after the dedication of the temple, Solomon appointed the courses of the priests and the levites to their charges, to praise and to minister before the priests, II. 8: 14. Here, again, while the charge of the music was handed over to the men, it did not confer upon them any distinction. It was no more than one of the means by which they praised and ministered, not before the Lord, but before the priests.

Finally, there remain a number of instances which can be referred to the original C, and in which the language employed, as in the above later passages, is more general. In them we hear no more of Asaph, Heman, and Jeduthun, or of guilds of musicians, but of levites who conducted the psalmody. Thus, on the occasion of Hezekiah's dedication of the temple the king set the levites there with cymbals, psalteries, and harps after the commandment of David, II. 29: 25; he also ordered the levites to sing with the words of David and of Asaph the seer, v. 30. During the following festival of Unleavened Bread the levites and the priests praised the Lord day by day with loud instruments, II. 30: 21. After the dedication and the festival Hezekiah settled the courses of the priests and levites for burnt-offerings and peace-offerings to minister and to give thanks and to praise, II. 31: 2. When, again, Josiah restored the temple, there is mention of levites who were overseers of the work, and of others who could skill of musical instruments, II. 34: 12, while at v. 13 appear a third body who were scribes, officers, and door-keepers. In the last instance it will be noted that the levites who were musicians were only a part of the whole body.

In view of this synopsis of the facts, it is at least an exaggeration to say that the function of the levites as singers was the specific interest which the Chronicler took in the men. Clearly the historian was interested in the temple-music, as he was interested in everything which concerned the cult. His narrative expands whenever he touches on the ritual. We could have little realization of the place which music occupied in the sacrificial worship, but for what he has told. Yet it is also true that any knowledge we possess as to the existence and the ritual of a dedication service in Israel is derived from his account. He also has described the method in which passover was celebrated, after the locus of that rite was changed from the homes of the people to the sanctuary. Any conclusions as to the alteration in the ritual which followed on this change must be based on his description of passover under Hezekiah and Josiah. C's interest in the musical part of the service is only an evidence of his interest in the cult generally.

The same thing is true about his association of the levites with the music. He certainly connected these clergy with the sacred song, but, as will be pointed out later, he assigned to the men much wider and more important functions. Their duties as singers were only one part of the service which they rendered, and these are not put forward prominently, as their right to carry the ark is emphasized.

Further, attention must be given to the fact that, in his description of conditions in the time of David, C was more careful in his use of language, and never wrote of the levites having been singers or musicians. He wrote of the men who were chosen from the larger class, either by the king or by their own chiefs, to fulfil this duty, or he described them by the names of their leaders. Only when he was dealing with the service under the later kings did he use looser language, which might appear to imply that the levites, as such, were charged with that duty; and even there, in connexion with Josiah's passover, he reverted to the stricter language which he had employed at the beginning. This means that, where he was dealing with the period when David determined the conditions which were to govern the future temple, he described the exact method by which the singers were decided; but, when he wrote about the later kings, he was content to say that these men restored the arrangements which had been made by David, and was not exact in his use of language on a minor feature of the service he described.

The attitude of the Chronicler in this matter can be readily understood, when it is seen in its historical setting. The developed musical service of the temple must have demanded a body of men who were possessed of a technical training. The lower duties about the sanctuary could be left to men who fulfilled them by rotation. When men were needed to act on any of the commissions of which there is mention under such kings as Jehoshaphat, those were chosen who had given proof of native ability or trained capacity. But a choral service which was a constant feature of the cult demanded a body of men who had received a special training for their duties. There had grown up, to answer this demand, the levitical guilds or choirs, and what the Chronicler did was to carry back this arrangement of his own time, and place it, as he placed so much else, under the authority of David.[1]

[1] In I Chr. c. 6 appears a passage, which, though it falls outside the scope of this study, deserves mention in a note. The chapter opens with a genealogy of Levi, vv. 1–15, and continues with a list of the levites whom David set over the service of song in the temple after the ark had rest, vv. 16–33. These men are said to have served in this capacity before the tabernacle of the tent of meeting until Solomon had built the temple, and to have fulfilled the duty כמשפטם, or according to the function allotted to them. The paragraph closes with the statement that their brethren the levites were נתונים or appointed for all the service of the tabernacle of the house of God. After this follows a description of the peculiar duties allotted to Aaron and his sons, vv. 34 ff.

The writer held the view that the temple took the place of the Mosaic tabernacle, and even insisted on it. He also made David's appointment of the levitical singers to their duties in the temple to be no novelty, but the continuation of an older arrangement which could claim a

B. The Levites and the Ark

There are certain other functions which the Chronicler attributed to the levites. The first of these which must be considered at some length was the right to carry the ark. In C's view they alone were capable of fulfilling this duty, which was not so much a task laid upon them as a privilege and an honour. When the author of Samuel recorded the successful transference of the ark, he merely stated that on this occasion the emblem was carried, as though by this means the stumble of the oxen which resulted in Uzzah's death was avoided. C, on the other hand, made David explain the earlier failure by the fact that the levites had not been the porters, and that thus the ordinance had not been observed. In this connexion we never hear of a guild who acted as porters of the ark: the privilege belonged to all the members of the tribe of Levi.

Accordingly, certain levites were selected to act as porters, and, as soon as the ark was deposited in the sanctuary which David had made ready for its reception, certain others were appointed to minister to it and to take charge of the choral service there. These last were members of the levitical sept who controlled the music. A regular cult was thus instituted in the sanctuary which David had erected in the capital he had won for his nation. The description of these events, which extends from I. 15: 4 to 16: 42 has not been left in its original form, but has been revised and considerably adapted, so that it must be examined in the hope that it may be possible to distinguish the elements of which it is composed.

higher authority, for the men held office in the tabernacle and were under a *mishpat* there. It is as though the writer had taken the occasion to develop the note of the annotator at I. 16: 39–42, who introduced the cult practised in the tabernacle at Gibeon into the story of David's institution of the cult before the ark. That tabernacle had been equipped with all the elements required for worship, for it possessed not only levitical singers, but levitical servitors. These last are described in terms which appear in the law of Exodus and Numbers: they were n'thoonim, given to the community, or given to the priests.

The passage begins by stating that David convened all Israel to take part in the solemn function, and continues with the further statement that he brought together the sons of Aaron and the levites, 15: 4–10. Here, already, it is remarkable that, while the sons of Aaron are left undefined as to their numbers or their classes, the levites are said to have comprised 872 men under 6 leaders.[1]

The king then summoned the leaders of these two bodies of clergy to receive instructions about the order of proceedings, and to make arrangements for the great event, v. 11 f. The leaders were Zadok and Abiathar on the part of the priests, and the six already mentioned chiefs on the part of the levites. But the mention of the priests, and especially of these two priests, is peculiarly unsuitable. For, when the king addressed the men he had summoned, he called them the heads of fathers' houses of the levites. Such a form of address was inappropriate for any priests, above all inappropriate in the case of Zadok, who at 12: 28 is called a נַעַר or youth. The word cannot be pressed too far, as though it necessarily implied one who had not yet reached manhood; but, when it is used in a wider sense than that of a youth, it is employed of one who was a subordinate. It could not well appear as the title of a leading priest, or of the head of a father's house. For these reasons I agree with Rothstein in regarding 'the priests' as an addition in vv. 4 and 11. The reviser found it intolerable to suppose that David passed over the higher clergy on such an occasion, the more intolerable because sacrifices were offered before the ark at the first stage of its journey, and to him sacrifices could only be offered by priests. He may even have been offended by the neglect of the Mosaic legislation which forbade the levites to handle any of the furniture of

---

[1] At v. 4 LXX[B] offers a very peculiar rendering, for it omits the *waw*, and reads 'the sons of Aaron the levites'. Such an expression, the levitical sons of Aaron, is unexampled, and its appearance at least suggests as the original the priests the levites, i.e. the levitical priests, a reading which is familiar elsewhere.

K

the tabernacle, including the ark, until the priests had wrapped up those sacred articles, cf. Num. 4: 15.

In its original form, therefore, the Chronicler's narrative made no reference here to the priests. When David resolved to bring the ark up to its new sanctuary, he summoned the levites for the purpose, and he issued instructions to these men as to their duties on the occasion. To notice, however, that the men needed such instructions and that they received these from the king suggests at least that the situation was unprecedented, and that neither king nor clergy had any accustomed rule to guide them. This compels us to look back and examine more closely the statement in v. 2 which inaugurated the whole movement. In R.V. this reads: 'none ought to carry the ark of God but the levites, for them hath the Lord chosen to carry the ark of God and to minister unto Him.' This has generally been taken to mean that David was careful to comply with the letter of the law as to the transport of the ark. For the terms of that law Rothstein and Benzinger have referred to Num. 1: 48–50, 3 : 5 ff., 4: 15, 7: 9, 10: 17. But these passages deal with the general question of the transport of the tabernacle and its furniture, and entrust that duty to the levites. None of them even mentions the ark, and one of them, 4: 15, forbids these clergy to touch any of the sacred articles, reserving this function to the priests. Now, if that law was the basis of David's action here, how could the ark be lifted at all, since only the priests might handle it? Further, if the *mishpat* which was followed was so old and so familiar, why did the men need careful instructions from the king in the method by which they were to carry out their duties?

The conclusion to which these facts lead is that v. 2 contains the promulgation of the rules which were to control the function, and that these rules were issued by the king. אָז אָמַר דָּוִד is the formal opening; then David decreed. The decree concerned the duties of the levites in relation to the ark, both on its journey and in its new sanctuary, and accordingly the king summoned the men into his presence. It also divided itself into two parts, of which the first was that only the levites were allowed to act as porters. Therefore he instructed the leading levites to make such arrangements as might meet and satisfy the new *mishpat*. But the more permanent part of the decree was that the Lord had commanded the levites not only to carry the ark but to minister unto it, not unto Him, for ever. Two considerations make it clear that this ministry was directed not unto God but unto the ark. On the one hand, if we follow Rothstein and suppose that here David was carrying out the regulations of the Mosaic period, he applied to the lower clergy a description of their office which is carefully avoided in that law. The Mosaic law called the levites ministers of the priests, ministers of the community, or ministers of the tabernacle; but it reserved the title of divine ministers to the priests. On the other hand, the interpretation offered above links up directly with the statement in 16: 4 that, as soon as it had reached its sanctuary, David appointed certain levites to minister unto the ark of God. He had provided for the first task of the transport: he now provided for the higher and more permanent duty of the cult. In connexion with both, he further took care for the provision of a choral service, and the conduct of that service was not entrusted to the levites as such, but to the trained guilds.[1]

---

[1] I have mentioned some of the positive reasons which point to the cult that was practised before the ark having consisted in more than a choral service. It may be legitimate to add here the negative criticism of the opposite opinion. The language used admits of a difference of judgement on the subject, for David is said to have appointed certain levites מְשָׁרְתִים וּלְהַזְכִּיר וּלְהוֹדוֹת וּלְהַלֵּל. Kittel, who limited the service to one of praise, was obliged to omit *waw* before the first verb without any authority from the text or from the versions. He then explained that the three verbs defined the preceding participle: the service of the levites consisted in celebrating and thanking and praising, where the three participles are mere variants. But it remains more than doubtful whether לְהַזְכִּיר, to celebrate, can be used in this general sense. The word appears in the headings of Psalms 38 and 70 in a technical direction,

Thus the initiative throughout was taken by the king. Such interference by the secular authority in matters which concerned the cult would have appeared intolerable to the later Judaism. To C, however, David was no ordinary king, for it was under divine direction that he planned the temple and laid down the lines of the worship there. While he did not actually build the house, he set up the sanctuary which preceded it, and in that first sanctuary at Jerusalem he was careful to include what remained permanent in the cult of Israel. Two things were essential to that worship, the ark, and the ministers who served it, the levites.

Accordingly it is natural to find that, when David committed the plans for the temple, which took the place of the tent at the old shrine, into the hands of Solomon and the leaders of the community, he charged them to transfer the ark and its sacred vessels to the new sanctuary, I. 22: 19. What follows that injunction was concerned with the levites, the age at which they entered on office, their courses and their duties. Again, C's account of the dedication of the temple related that the levites brought the ark into the new building and offered sacrifice before it. Thereupon the glory of the Lord filled the house, for the sanctuary was accepted, when it was built before an altar, the site of which had been indicated by a theophany, and when it contained

which is more naturally understood to refer to the use of the two psalms in connexion with a particular ritual. It differs very markedly from similar technical headings to other psalms, which refer to the musical accompaniment. This explanation is strengthened by the use of the word in Isa. 66: 3, where the verb is coupled with incense, and cannot mean anything else except some form of sacrifice. The root, again, appears in the אַזְכָּרָה, which was definitely a sacrificial term, cf. Lev. 2: 2, 9, 16; 5: 12; 6: 8; Num. 5: 26.

It has been necessary to add this note, because I cannot dispose of the question of this service before the ark by the easy method of saying that in early Israel a cult, which consisted of no more than a service of praise, was inconceivable. We are not dealing with primitive usage, but with the ideas of the Chronicler on the worship he ascribed to David.

the ark and the servitors whom David had appointed,[1] II. 5: 2–6.

Temple, ark, and levites appear in combination for the last time in the preface with which C introduced his account of Josiah's passover, II. 35: 1–4. The king addressed the levites as to their duties at the approaching celebration, calling them the teachers of all Israel and holy unto the Lord. In itself it is remarkable that he should have described the men at all, but still more remarkable are the terms which he applied to them. Both expressions magnify their office in language which has no direct relation to the passover, and both assign to them a dignity which the later law reserved to the priests. Only the Deuteronomic law, the Chronicler in his accounts of Jehoshaphat's reform, and the author of Neh. 8: 7–9[2] entrusted the teaching of the law to the levites. Again, the men are said to be holy unto the Lord here and at II. 23: 6: in the later law this dignity was reserved to the priests.[3]

Josiah then bade the men who were thus qualified for their task to put the holy ark into the house which Solomon the son of David did build, there shall no more be a burden upon your shoulders. The command is difficult to interpret, and has given rise to considerable discussion as well as to some far-reaching conclusions. The first difficulty is to explain why it was necessary to issue any order about depositing in the temple an emblem which had been brought into it at the time of its dedication. The second is to see why the temple was said to have been built by Solomon the son of David, as though there were any other. Any explanation, which is to be entirely satisfactory, must meet and answer both questions. Benzinger proposed to meet the first difficulty by reading הִנֵּה instead of תְּנוּ, which gave him the reading 'behold the holy ark is in the temple'; but he does not appear even to have recognized the second. Kittel,

---

[1] For the analysis of the passage, cf. pp. 37 ff.

[2] Cf. the discussion of this passage in my *Post-Exilic Judaism*, pp. 262 ff.

[3] Cf. *HDB*. iv. 93.

again, in *B.H.* has suggested מְנוּחַת for תְּנוּ אֶת, which may be translated 'the holy ark is at rest' in the temple, for which he compared I. 28: 2. The clause gives bad Hebrew, but not much worse than C wrote elsewhere. A third suggestion may be ventured based on a LXX rendering which appears in I Esdras. The Greek ἐν τῇ θέσει may answer to כָּתַת in place of תְּנוּ or תְּנוּ אֶת, and the clause might then read: 'since the holy ark was deposited in Solomon's temple, there has been no further occasion for it to be carried.' Either this rendering or that proposed by Kittel explains why the temple is called 'the house which Solomon the son of David king of Israel did build'. The writer was referring to the dedication service which, since its central feature was the deposition of the ark, exempted the levites from any further need to act as its porters. Whether, however, either emendation is accepted or the present text is retained, there remains an insistence on the sacred character of the ark, on its continued presence in the temple, and on the connexion of the levites with it. The retention of the present text lays emphasis on the privilege of the levites as its porters.

'Now,' continued the king, 'serve the Lord your God and His people Israel, and prepare yourselves after your fathers' houses by your courses according to the writing of David king of Israel, and according to the writing of Solomon his son.' Since their privilege of acting as porters to the ark had come to an end, the levites were free to undertake new duties. These functions involved higher responsibilities, for they were to serve the Lord and His people Israel. But, according to the later law, it was the priests who were privileged to serve the Lord and the people: the function of the levites was to serve the priests. For proof of this it is only necessary to refer to the passage which described the investment of the levites in their office: 'the Lord spake unto Moses, saying, bring the tribe of Levi near and set them before Aaron the priest, that they may minister unto him', Num. 3: 5 f.

This procedure on Josiah's part is described immediately

before the celebration of the passover, but it has a wider, more general reference than merely to that event. The king aimed at restoring the conditions which had prevailed in the temple when it was built. Hence he dwelt on the fact that the ark had been there since the time of Solomon. But that emblem had no connexion with the festival of passover. Again he bade the levites prepare themselves in their courses according to the directions of David. Yet any such instructions could offer no guidance for the men's conduct at a passover which had not been kept by any of the kings of Israel. Again, the description of the levites as the teachers of all Israel had no connexion with the duties they were required to perform at the festival. Thus the introductory verses, while they immediately precede the description of Josiah's passover, describe arrangements which were not confined to that event, and were not designed merely to prepare for it. They form a species of preface which defined certain permanent arrangements that were made by the reforming king.

That this was the case becomes clearer when we compare the statement of the Chronicler with another passage which, though distant in date, is very similar in substance, I. 23: 24 ff. The passage occurs in the long description of the instructions David gave to his successor, and forms the conclusion of a section which bears on the duties and the courses of the levites. The chapter is plainly not homogeneous, but derives from at least two authors: and the conclusion with which we are concerned here has been introduced by a reviser.[1] This writer began by describing the levites in long, somewhat cumbrous phrases, which are reminiscent of similar language on the same subject in the Book of Numbers,[2] but he omitted all reference to their division into classes, which was the subject of the preceding paragraph. Instead of this, he stated that from this period in the national history one duty which had devolved on the levites had

[1] For the proof of this statement, cf. p. 85 f.
[2] Cf. Num. 1: 2, &c.

come to an end. Since God had given Israel rest, and since
He Himself had taken up His abode in Jerusalem, there was
no further need for them to carry the tabernacle and its
vessels.[1] Henceforth their duties were concerned with the
temple and its cult, and, while their status was alongside the
priests, it was definitely subordinate to that of the higher
clergy.[2] To them also was committed all responsibility for the
choral service, but here, as at II. 5:12, this charge occurs
in a passage which dwelt, not on the dignity, but on the
inferiority of the levites. As for their share in the sacrifices,
it was carefully limited. Everything which they performed
there must be כְּמִשְׁפָּט עֲלֵיהֶם, within the regulations which
were laid down for them, or according to the prevailing use.
Finally, their function in general was to serve the tabernacle
and the holy place and the sons of Aaron their brethren.

These directions are so closely parallel to the paragraph
which has been reviewed that it is impossible to deny some
relation between them. And that relation can only be that
the words put into the mouth of David were intended, not
to supplement, but to correct the utterances of Josiah, and
to counteract their dangerous implications. The reviser
could not, in this case, appeal to the authority of the Mosaic
legislation, as he did elsewhere. He employed the same
method to which he had recourse in attempting to reconcile
the divergence between the 30 years of v. 3 and the 20 years
of v. 24 at which the levites entered on office, and called his
addition David's last words. The final decision of the king,
v. 27, had been for 20 years of age, and his final decision on
the status of the levites had been as it was defined in the law.
When Josiah referred the levites to the writings of David
and Solomon, it must be understood that he meant the last
message of the great king.

The comparison of these two crucial passages has revealed
the same double strand in the Chronicler's narrative which

---

[1] Cf. Num. 3: 7 ff. and chap. 4.

[2] The details given about those duties, as Rothstein has pointed out,
are based on Lev. c. 2.

became apparent in the study of David's relation to the temple. To C the temple took the place of the tent which housed the ark, and the ark itself was the central and essential feature in both tent and temple. Therefore, also, the levites, whom David appointed to serve the ark in its tent, held a leading place in the cult of the temple. The reviser, on the other hand, regarded the temple as having taken the place of the tabernacle. The leading feature of the cult at the tabernacle was its altar, at which the priests were alone competent to offer sacrifice. Therefore these priests held complete authority over the cult, where they served the Lord and Israel, while the levites in turn served them. As for the ark, it had been merely part of the furniture of the tabernacle, and it occupied no higher position in the temple. It was relegated to obscurity in the inner shrine, and any sanctity it possessed or reverence it could claim was not inherent in itself, but was due to the fact of its containing the tablets of the law.

C. Other Functions Assigned to the Levites

The responsibility of the levites for the choral service and their relation to the ark did not exhaust the Chronicler's interest in this body of the clergy. He regarded, as falling within their competence, certain other duties which differ in character from those which have been passed in review. The choral service and the ministry of the ark were directly connected with the cult and were confined by C to the levites. The functions, which must now be detailed, extended beyond the temple and brought the men into contact with other sides of the national life. They were also not confined to the levites, but were shared with other members of the community.

C credited his reforming kings with an interest in the welfare of their nation, which was not confined to fostering the worship in the temple. From him we hear of the appointment of certain royal commissions which were charged with the duty of improving conditions in the kingdom. In all of

L

these levites took a part, sometimes a leading part. The
first mention of such a commission is also in some respects
the most remarkable. Jehoshaphat is said to have appointed
five princes, nine levites, and two priests to teach in Judah,
having the book of the law of the Lord with them, II. 17: 7–9.
In his note on the passage Kittel was almost entirely concerned with the historical question as to whether it was
possible to suppose that a book of the law existed at that
early date, but he did draw attention to the feature that a
commission charged with such a duty was said to have contained a large proportion of laymen.

Since our inquiry is not concerned with the historical
question, what concerns us most in the statement is the composition of the royal commission. The levites were not only
entrusted with the task of teaching the law—there are other
passages which assign that duty to them—but they constituted the majority on a body of men, to whom the duty
was assigned. The same king is credited by C with having
initiated measures in the direction of improving the administration of justice in his kingdom. One part of that reform
consisted in the appointment of a high court of appeal at
Jerusalem, II. 19: 5 ff. Here Kittel has proposed a slight
emendation of the text at the close of v. 8, which gives sense
to an otherwise meaningless sentence. The MT reads
לְמִשְׁפַּט יהוה וְלָרִיב וַיָּשֻׁבוּ יְרוּשָׁלִָם, which makes the king set up
the court in Jerusalem 'for the judgement of the Lord and
for controversies. And they returned to Jerusalem'. As,
however, the court was to have its seat in the city, the last
sentence offers no sense. Kittel reads for the last five words
לְמִשְׁפָּטֵי or לְמִשְׁפַּט יהוה וּלְרִיבֵי יֹשְׁבֵי יְרוּשָׁלִָם, and makes them
define the scope of the new court. It was set up in the capital
in order to deal with the religious affairs of the general community and with the secular concerns of the inhabitants of
Jerusalem. This supreme court was to consist of Levites,
priests, and heads of fathers' houses in *Israel*. When it dealt
with the religious questions which were referred to it, its
president was to be the high-priest: when royal affairs were

under consideration, it was presided over by the prince of the house of *Israel*. The שֹׁטְרִים or executive officers were again levites. Thus the levites fulfilled a double function in the court of final instance. They constituted the officials who were charged with carrying out its decisions, but they also formed part of the court itself; and, when they appear in the latter capacity, they are again mentioned first. The significance of the functions which are ascribed to the men can only be fully recognized when the passages which describe Jehoshaphat's commission for teaching the law and his institution of a supreme court are thus set together. C claimed that the levites were competent to instruct the people in the divine law, and to sit on the court of appeal which decided on cases which dealt with that law.

It is no concern of the present study to attempt to decide on the historical accuracy of the measures of reform which are here ascribed to Jehoshaphat. The fact that he made the court consist in part of heads of fathers' houses in Israel, and that he called its president in certain cases the prince of the house of Israel, may be held to suggest that C forgot that he was describing action taken by a king of Judah. He may, therefore, have been dealing with conditions which emerged and arrangements which were made during the period after the Return. But, if that be held to be the situation, it only makes the attitude he took more remarkable. For then, at a time when the levites were being relegated to a definitely subordinate status, he described these lower clergy as fully competent to teach and to administer the divine law.[1]

In connexion with the repairs in the temple, which were carried out by Joash, our two sources differ so widely that

[1] Benzinger held that the visitation described in these verses was the same as that already described in 17: 7–9. But the appointment of judges throughout the Judean towns is not parallel to that of a commission whose business it was to teach the divine law in the kingdom. The court set up in the capital had nothing to do with the teaching of the law: it had to deal with the way in which that law was observed. Nor did Benzinger explain why, if the case was as he supposed, the account was duplicated.

the account in Chronicles amounts to a complete recasting of that in Kings.[1] What concerns us here is that, according to C, the money devoted to the purpose was brought for royal inspection through or under the hand of the levites. They were made responsible for the supervision of the collection. Again, in preparation for the rededication of the temple after its desecration by Ahaz, Hezekiah summoned the priests and levites into one of the city plazas. The king, however, only addressed the levites, and in his charge to them bade them not to be negligent because the Lord had chosen them to stand before Him, to minister unto Him, and that they should be His ministers and burn incense, II. 29: 3–11. The functions here ascribed to the men are described in terms which were reserved to the priests in the later law. It is accordingly remarkable, if not suspicious, to find that v. 16, which describes the fulfilment of the royal command, declares that it was carried out by the priests to whom Hezekiah gave no charge on the subject.[2] Hezekiah, further, made arrangements for the support of the temple clergy, ordering the people who lived in Jerusalem to make provision for the priests and the levites in order that they might be free to devote themselves to the divine law, II. 31: 4. The two classes of officials were thus placed on an equal footing, alike in relation to their claim for support and in the duties which they were to be left free to fulfil. The king also ordered rooms to be prepared for storing these offerings, and entrusted the care of these to the levites, v. 11. Finally, when Josiah restored the temple he committed the task of collecting the necessary funds to the same men, who supervised as well the work and the workmen, II. 34: 9.

In all these cases the Chronicler was dealing with the work of kings who were reformers and who were commended by him as such; and all of them gave peculiar prominence to the levites as assistants in the aims they had

[1] For an analysis of II Chr. 24: 4–16, cf. p. 78 f.

[2] For a full examination of the passage cf. the chapter on Hezekiah's Reform.

at heart. They were more numerous than the priests on
the commission which Jehoshaphat appointed to teach the
divine law, and they held a position of equal authority on
the final court of appeal which dealt with the administration
of the law. They were given the leading part at the purification and rededication of the temple by Hezekiah. Under
the same king they had a share in the collection of the
dues devoted to the maintenance of the temple clergy, they
benefited along with the priests from this provision, and to
them was committed the responsibility for supervising and
distributing the offerings after they had been collected.
Josiah continued the last practice and committed to the men
the collection of the funds for the restoration of the temple
and the supervision of their expenditure.

In a number of instances the levites were associated with
the priests in these duties and benefits, but, except that the
high-priest presided over the supreme court at Jerusalem in
religious issues, there is no hint that they were subordinate
to their brethren. Since, however, the functions which have
formed the subject of our last section are concerned with
matters not directly connected with the cult, it might be
possible to conclude that C confined his view of the equality
of the two orders to everything which did not touch the
actual cult. But there remain three clear indications that
he made the equality absolute. Before the dedication of the
temple, he put into the mouth of Hezekiah an exhortation
in which the king bade the levites be diligent because they
were the elect of God, to stand before Him, to minister unto
Him, to be His ministers and to burn incense, II. 29: 11.
After the passover and festival of unleavened bread under
the same king he stated that the priests the levites arose and
blessed the people, II. 30: 27. He made Josiah give instructions to the levites that now they were to serve the Lord
their God and His people Israel, II. 35: 3. These are titles
and functions which the later law reserved to the priests.

EXCURSUS ON II Chr. 24: 4–14

This passage, which describes the arrangements made by Joash
for the repair of the temple, has a parallel in II Kings 12: 5–17;
but, while the Chronicler used the earlier narrative, he did not
so much follow as entirely recast it.[1] According to K, the king
instituted measures for the repairs without any reference to the
damage which the sanctuary or its furniture had sustained at the
hands of Athaliah. If we possessed only K's account, it would
be natural to conclude that Joash had in view some permanent
arrangement for maintaining the sacred building, by setting apart
certain revenues which accrued to it, in order to defray the necessary expenses for its repair. Whether his motive was to relieve
the royal exchequer or to make sure that the condition of the
temple was not dependent on the whim of the king, must remain
uncertain. The exact source of these funds is far from clear,
for v. 5, in which they are defined, has the appearance of being
conflate: but they were plainly not new charges, imposed upon
the worshippers for the first time. They had been paid into the
temple treasury before the time of Joash, and were now to be
diverted to serve a special purpose. It is, accordingly, possible that
Kittel's suggestion is correct, and that the money from these consecrated things and from voluntary offerings was part of the permanent revenue of the temple-priesthood. What Joash proposed,
on that view, was that these funds should henceforth meet the expenses of the temple repairs, as well as help to meet the needs of
the priests. The royal proposal came to nothing because of the successful resistance of the clerical order. The exact way in which the
men defeated this attack on their rights is not clear. They may
simply have refused to surrender their claim to the offerings, or they
may have declined to accept any of this money from the worshippers, either for themselves or for the repairs, and so have brought
matters to a deadlock. At least it was only after the failure of his
first proposal that Joash was forced to have recourse to another
method. He set up an offertory-box beside the altar inside the
temple and appealed directly to the laity. When the box was full
the king's secretary and the chief-priest took charge of the money
and distributed it for the purpose for which it had been given.

C, on the other hand, began by the statement that the need for
repairs was due to the damage which Athaliah had done to the
temple, its fabric and its furniture. Accordingly he omitted all
reference to the royal proposal to charge the cost of the repairs on

[1] Kittel's note is here of peculiar value.

the ordinary revenues of the sanctuary, and he was equally silent about the resistance of the priests in the matter. Since the necessity was due to a temporary cause, it could be met by a contribution *ad hoc*. Joash met the situation by a direct appeal to the worshippers, and, after due proclamation of his purpose, set up the offertory-box. Since, however, the laity were no longer admitted within the precincts of the temple, C was careful to state that the box was set up outside. When it was full it was brought in by the levites and emptied by the king's scribe and the high-priest's officer.

This original account of C has been supplemented by an annotator, who added vv. 5 and 6. That the verses are an addition is plain from several indications. Thus they break the close connexion between v. 4 and v. 7. Verse 7 begins 'for Athaliah, the miscreant, had wrecked the temple', and thus explains why Joash in v. 4 'was minded to restore the house of the Lord'. The statement has no connexion with the royal question to the high-priest in v. 6 about the delay in the collection of the levy. Further, the intruded verses relate the appointment of a royal commission to raise a levy for the temple repairs in the towns of Judah. The substance of this, except for one addition, is repeated in v. 9. There, after the offertory-box had been set up at the temple-gate, Joash issued a proclamation to explain its purpose. The purpose is stated to have been to receive the assessed tax which was due for the temple from every Israelite. What, then, had become of the commission which was charged with the collection of this assessment? Were they simply dissolved because some of their number, the levites, had been slow in the performance of their duty? In that case the offertory-box was something to which Joash resorted when his commissioners failed to perform their task. Yet it becomes difficult to explain why one body of these men showed themselves thus reluctant. In Kings the author was careful to state that Joash's final expedient was due to reluctance on the part of the priests, and even suggested a cause for their unwillingness. No reason is even offered for the slowness of the levites.

The presence of a later hand is generally acknowledged here, and the reason for his interference has been explained by his desire to exonerate the priesthood from the slur which was cast upon them in K's account. But it must always appear a very curious procedure on the part of an annotator that he left untouched the original document, in which the slur appeared, and added a note to another document which contained no hint of any aspersion on the conduct of the priests. It is much more probable that the writer wished to supplement the narrative in C. The young and pious king, who was guided by the high-priest in his early life, could not have ignored the Mosaic practice in any measures he took for the restoration of the temple. He had revived the levy which Moses laid upon the people in the wilderness when he set up and equipped the tabernacle, Exod. 30: 11–16, 38: 25 f.; and, when he set up the offertory-box it was to receive, not the voluntary gifts of the faithful, but the assessment from the people, which was to 'be a memorial for the children of Israel before the Lord, to make atonement for their souls'. At the same time as the annotator thus made Joash act in obedience to the Mosaic law, he was able to insist on his favourite theme, that the temple had taken the place of the tabernacle in the wilderness.

There is a minor point of difference between the two accounts, which amounts to a direct contradiction. While K stated that the money collected was enough to meet the cost of the repairs, he added that none of it was employed to provide for sacred vessels. The contributions were reserved for the one end which had been in view from the beginning. The remark tallies with Kittel's view that in Kings Joash was aiming at the provision of a permanent means of providing a fund for the maintenance of the temple fabric. It was not intended to cover any charges for the renewal of the sacred vessels. On the other hand, the passage in Chronicles states definitely that, 'when they had made an end, they brought the rest of the money before the king and Jehoiada, whereof were made vessels for the house of the Lord', v. 14a. The statement is more than awkward in its present position; for it follows the remark that the king and the high-priest distributed the money from the box to the workmen who were engaged in the repairs, and that these men had completed their task, so that the sanctuary was set up in its state. When the work was done they offered burnt-offerings there continually all the days of Jehoiada, v. 14b. There is no hint of any surplus which could be spent on the provision of sacred vessels. Again, it is natural to recognize the hand of the annotator, who was making the incident conform to the account in Exodus; for the assessment which Moses levied on the people in the wilderness had defrayed the cost of the furniture in the tabernacle as well as that of its fabric. He found the point of attachment for his addition in the earlier statement of C, according to which, in the time of Athaliah, the temple had been wrecked and its sacred vessels had been devoted to the service of the baal sanctuary. These were not worthy to be used again in the temple.[1]

---

[1] This direct contradiction between the two sources is explained differently and very ingeniously by Bertheau.

IV

ANALYSIS OF I CHR. CHAPTERS 23-6

THESE chapters profess to give the arrangements made by David as to the officials who were responsible for the oversight of the future temple and for the conduct of the worship there. The men are grouped under the headings of levites, priests, and door-keepers; and special attention is devoted to the division of the officials into classes, apparently in order to regulate the system according to which they were to undertake the duties assigned to them. The material is extremely confused, so confused that in certain cases it defies, in my judgement, every effort to bring it into order. Clearly it is also not homogeneous, but bears evidence of having been derived from several hands. How many of these later hands were at work, and whether it is possible to decide in each case their aim in supplementing the original, are questions which remain hard to decide. While it is possible to detect certain broad lines of division on which a student may pronounce with some confidence, there are other conclusions which he must confess to be merely tentative.

The want of unity in authorship appears in the opening chapter, for the same writer cannot be held responsible for the statement in v. 3 that the levites entered on office at 30 years of age, and for that in vv. 24 and 27 which gave the age as 20.

So large a change in the age at which the men assumed their functions points to an alteration in the conditions of the community which demanded a reduction in the age-limit. The suspicion that in vv. 24 and 27 we have to do with a later hand is increased by the fact of those verses being prefaced by a somewhat lengthy description of the levites, which was uncalled for in the circumstances, after the men had been introduced in v. 2 without any such

M

description. Then it becomes of interest to notice that the
reviser was careful to put the lower age of the levites among
the last acts or words of David, v. 27. He could not fail to
be conscious of the discrepancy, and he explained it by
ascribing the 30 years' limit to the king's early life and the
other to his mature period. Since the low age was David's
final charge to his son, it was the decision which governed
the use of the temple.

Accordingly Kittel made vv. 6–24 later than what precedes. He then took the list of names in vv. 7–23 to indicate
the classes or courses into which David, according to v. 6,
divided the levites. Now in the second temple the levites
were divided into twenty-four such classes, and it was
natural to expect this arrangement to have been credited
to the king. Since, however, the list does not contain twenty-
four names of men who were heads of fathers' houses in Levi,
various efforts have been made to bring about the desired
correspondence. Curtis has given a list of these attempts,[1]
and added his own. He believed he could discover twenty-
three names, and suggested that the twenty-fourth has
dropped out. But the variety of the expedients offered and
the forced character of some of them do not give much confidence in the result. They rather raise the question whether
the list of names was intended originally to supply the heads
of the levitical courses; and a closer examination of the
verses reveals that what they contain is a genealogy of Levi
under the three branches of Gershon, vv. 7–11, Kohath,
vv. 12–20, and Merari, vv. 21–3. The genealogy is well connected, except at vv. 13 f.,[2] and is nowhere brought down to
the period of David, as becomes evident when it is compared
with similar genealogies elsewhere, as in Num. 3: 17 ff.;
I Chr. 5: 27 ff., 6: 1 ff. Yet the men whom David appointed
to be leaders of the levitical courses must have been his contemporaries. Nor is this all, for the line of descent in the
three clans does not appear to be followed out to the same

[1] In his commentary I.C.C. *ad loc.*
[2] On this cf. p. 85.

stage, so that the last names in the list are not necessarily contemporaries of one another.

This curious feature in the list of names in chap. 23 makes a student turn to the similar list of the descendants of Levi, which appears in 24: 20-30. This is headed 'as to the other or the rest of the sons of Levi', and so is brought into connexion with the list in chap. 23: the two passages are also connected in subject and content. But a closer comparison of the two brings to light another, more remarkable relation between them. For 24: 20 carries the genealogy of 23: 12 f., 15 f., a stage further, adding, as it does, the name of Shubael's son to 23: 16. Verse 21 does the same for 23: 17, giving Rehabyah's son.[1] Verse 22 adds a son of Shelomith, while v. 23 is a mere repetition of 23: 19. Verses 24 f., again, bring the genealogy of Uzziel in its two branches, 23: 20, a stage further. Verse 26a repeats 23: 21a, and 26b must be corrupt, since it cannot be reconciled with the terms of v. 27. Two suggestions for its emendation have been offered,[2] each of which has the same result of making v. 27 carry the descent of Merari a stage further. Verse 28 repeats 23: 22 in an abbreviated form, while v. 29 adds a son of Kish to 23: 21. Finally, v. 30a is a repetition of 23: 23, and v. 30b reproduces the first clause of 23: 24.

The rubric which heads the second list, as to the remaining sons of Levi, may have been intended to mark that it was supplementary to its predecessor, and the fact of its bringing down the levitical genealogy into another generation may appear to support such a conclusion. The remaining sons of Levi could, though with some difficulty, be taken to refer to these additional names. But there is another feature of the list prefaced by those words, which presents a difficulty. The list of chap. 24 has seriously curtailed that of chap. 23, since it does not concern itself with all the branches of the tribe of Levi: it made no mention of the Gershonites, and confined its attention to the Kohathites and Merarites.

[1] Cf. 26: 25.
[2] By Kittel and Curtis.

Whatever be the explanation of these facts, this comparison between the two lists makes it impossible to suppose that their original purpose was to supply the representative levites whom David divided into courses. He could not have both included and excluded the Gershonites: nor could he have set over his courses at the same time a body of men and their sons.

It must next be noted that neither of the lists is integrally related to the preceding context in which it appears. Both begin with a similar rubric, לבני לוי in the one case, הנותרים in the other. The similarity of the headings is not apparent in the R.V., which has translated the two prepositions differently in order to make some connexion with what precedes. In reality there is no such connexion: the ל, like על in other cases,[1] merely introduced an independent document, and is best translated with a capital: Concerning the sons of Levi, or Concerning the other sons of Levi: then followed the genealogy.

This implies in turn that the opening clause of v. 6, 'and David divided them into courses', originally had no connexion with what follows, but formed the conclusion of the preceding five verses.

The opening paragraph belongs to the Chronicler and connects closely with his representation of the situation. He made David summon the leaders of Israel and address them before his death. The charge closed with a command to build the temple and to bring the ark with its vessels into it. When, therefore, C continued with an account of David's arrangements as to the temple officials, he began with the men whom the king had appointed to serve the ark. He made David bring the men together, number them, determine the age at which they entered on their functions, and distribute them into the courses after which they were to fulfil their duties. But he did not feel it necessary to tell who the levites were, as is done in v. 24. Their place in the future temple was well

---

[1] Compare Neh. 10: 2, where על introduces a list of names, and Jer. 23: 9, where ל precedes a collection of oracles.

known. On the other hand, the earlier list of names has been brought into integral relation to what follows. This connexion must be due to the later hand, since the age at which the levites entered on their duty is set down at 20 years. The writer felt it necessary to characterize the men, and he employed for the purpose language which is reminiscent of the terms used about the levites in the book of Numbers. This description led on naturally to the last paragraph of the chapter, vv. 25-32. Certain aspects of this section have already been discussed.[1] Here it only remains to add that the writer entirely departed from the subject, which was stated in v. 6a. Instead of dealing with the levitical courses, he turned his attention to a careful definition of the relation between priest and levite. Probably the same hand was responsible for introducing vv. 13b, 14, into the list of names which he incorporated into his account. In its original form as a genealogy of Levi, the remark there that the sons of Amram were Moses and Aaron was equally true and innocuous. But when the genealogy was turned into a list of the fathers' houses of the levites, on which list their courses were based, it became dangerous, since it included Aaron among the levites. Accordingly the reviser added a note to the effect that, while Aaron was by descent a levite, by function he was a priest.

In my judgement it is impossible to determine the source of the two genealogies of Levi, as impossible as in the case of the similar lists of I. 5: 27, 6: 1. The reviser found them and used them for his purpose of describing the courses of the levites. A similar case of his use of alien material for the same end occurs later.[2]

In chap. 24, vv. 1-19 form a single block, which deals with the courses of the priests. The author connected this distribution with the time of David, and so made it clear that the arrangement he described had existed in the temple from the beginning. At v. 3, however, he was careful to state that the king was not alone in the matter, but acted in con-

---

[1] Cf. pp. 71 ff.   [2] Cf. p. 88.

currence with Zadok and Ahimelech, the representatives of the two legitimate branches of the Aaronic priesthood. He further added that the settlement made by the king was not only acceptable to his leading priests, but was in itself no novelty, since it followed an ordinance revealed by God to Aaron, v. 19.[1] The order followed by the priests in their courses had existed in the temple during all its history, but it had, before the temple came into existence, been in force in the tabernacle. It was thus possessed of a higher authority than that of David. The paragraph reflects the situation at the period of the Return, for every commentator who has dealt with the list of courses has noted that many of the names which appear in it reappear in Ezra, and to an even greater extent in Nehemiah.

The more interesting and perplexing features in the passage appear, not in the list, but in the verses by which it has been prefaced, vv. 1b–6. These give the impression of the preface having been framed in view of a particular historical situation, even to meet a historical problem. Thus the author went a little out of his way to introduce the story of the rejection of the two priestly clans, Nadab and Abihu, for the sin of offering strange fire.[2] Why was it felt necessary to refer to the expulsion of two clans in connexion with a statement on the courses of the priesthood? Again, the reservation of the priestly dignity to the families of Eleazar and Ithamar, with special stress laid on the predominance of the line of Eleazar, from which Zadok was descended, is at least peculiar in the same connexion. The combination of the two statements, one of which reserved the priestly office to two families, while the other defined the relative dignity of those two, suggests that the conditions of the writer's time made the decision of the constitution of the

---

[1] There is no ordinance which refers to this specific question in the present Pentateuch.

[2] The account in v. 2 is abridged from Num. 3: 4; cf. the longer account in Lev. 10: 1 ff. Both these records are embedded in the law and do not appear in the general history.

higher clergy imperative. The use of the lot in the matter
may even indicate that it became necessary to seek a divine
decision, and this may point to an impasse having been
reached which could be resolved in no other way. Finally,
the distinction between princes of the sanctuary and princes
of God, coupled with the remark that men of the two types
were found in both lines of the Aaronic priesthood, points
in the same direction. The fact that the meaning of the
distinction has been entirely lost again suggests a historical
situation in the affairs of the community. When a settlement
was reached which reconciled the contending interests or
opinions, even the memory of what caused the difficulty
disappeared.

Now the only period at which we hear of division between
two bodies of priests in old Israel is that which followed the
Return, when the relative claims of the priests who had
never been in exile and of those who had come back from
Babylon required to be adjusted. I have already pointed
out that Joshua's right to the high priesthood was not at
once acknowledged, but was seriously questioned.[1] I suggest
that the present passage contains an echo of the same debate.
If we may interpret it along these lines, it explains why the
line of Eleazar, from which the family of Zadok claimed
descent, received the higher position here. We know that
the leading priests at the temple were deported by Nebuchadrezzar, and, while we cannot accept the large numbers
of those who returned according to the book of Ezra, we may
venture to conclude that the descendants of these men had
stronger motives to return than the rest of the exiles. As
Joshua was restored to the high priesthood, the men of his
family may have obtained a double representation in the
cult service. Before the writer here set down the allocation
of the priestly courses in the temple, he indicated the basis
on which the allocation was made.

In the conclusion of the chapter the same writer, instead
of making David decide on the levitical courses as in 23: 6a,

[1] In *Post-Exilic Judaism*, chap. x.

made the levites cast lots for this allocation and made this take place in the presence of David, the leading priests, and the leading levites, v. 31. He there introduced the second genealogy. The passage presents three unanswerable problems. Why did the author, who had given a list of twenty-four names as heads of the priestly courses, not even attempt to give twenty-four names of leading levites? Why did he carry the genealogy which he included one stage lower than the earlier one? And why did he ignore the line of Gershon? These questions, it may be added, are equally urgent and difficult to answer, if his list of names is not regarded as a genealogy.

At a first reading chap. 25 appears to follow naturally on what has preceded. After the description of the courses into which the priests and levites were divided, came the similar division of the singers. The formal unity, indeed, might seem to be better preserved here than it is in the other cases, since in vv. 7–21 the number of the singers is set down as 288, distributed into 24 courses, each of which consisted of 12 men. Now vv. 1–6 enumerate 24 descendants of the leading singers, Asaph, Heman, and Jeduthun,[1] and these 24, when multiplied by 12, give the 288 who were distributed among the courses in the later section.

But Benzinger and Kittel have drawn attention to the fact that the remark at the close of v. 1 as to the number of those who did the work according to their service is an intrusion. For that number does not emerge until v. 7, where it forms the basis for the distribution of the men into courses. Curtis wished to retain the clause and refer the number to the descendants of Asaph, Heman, and Jeduthun in vv. 2–6, while he referred the number in v. 7 to the following 288. But an examination of vv. 2–6 has disclosed that a number of the names which profess to be those of sons of Heman are impossible as proper names: they really compose the verse of a prayer which invoked the divine

[1] Reading at the close of v. 3, with LXX[BA], the Shimei mentioned in v. 17, instead of 'six', the version of M.T. and R.V.

mercy.[1] Verses 2-6 did not originally contain twenty-four names.

When this is recognized, certain other conclusions follow. The writer who enumerated the 24 courses of the singers understood the earlier verses to contain a list of names, for he made them the basis of his series. Evidently, then, he was making use of older material, in which the brief prayer was already incorporated. Again, the correspondence between the numbers in the first list and those in the second disappears. Originally there were not present the 24 names which, when multiplied by 12, give the total of 288. The relation between the two sections must be acknowledged to be artificial, and the clause in v. 1, to which Benzinger and Kittel took exception, is the work of a reviser whose aim was to link up his borrowed material with his list of the courses of the levitical singers.[2]

The chapter, then, is not homogeneous. After the work of the reviser has been sifted out, his purpose becomes clear. He made use of older material in order to form the basis for his division of the levitical singers into 24 courses, as he used the genealogies of Levi for his classification of the ordinary levites. In both cases he appears to have gravely misunderstood the character of the material which he incorporated in his own account. But his aim was to distribute the priests, the levites, and the singers into the courses which became necessary in the cult after the Return. There remain the opening six verses, from which must be omitted the final clauses of vv. 1 and 5. According to this, David and the captains of the host, without any assistance from Zadok and Ahimelech, appointed certain of the sons of Asaph, Heman, and Jeduthun, whose task it was to prophesy with harps, with psalteries, and with cymbals. This is not exactly

---

[1] For the reconstruction cf. Rothstein in his Commentary, and Haupt, *ZAW.* 1914, pp. 42 ff.

[2] Further evidence in the same direction may be found in Rothstein's note on v. 9. In this he has shown the difficulty, in my judgement the impossibility, of connecting that verse with vv. 1-6.

parallel to the king's act after he had brought the ark into Jerusalem, I 15: 16. There he provided for the choral service in the new sanctuary by instructing the levitical leaders to set apart some of their number to act as singers. Thereupon the leaders selected Asaph, Heman, and Jeduthun to superintend that service. The present passage described a further development, in which neither the men set apart for the duty nor the function to which they were set apart were the same. Only certain members of the choral guilds were chosen here, and their task was to prophesy with musical accompaniment. These features of the account are sufficient to make it evident that the passage did not merely imply the appointment of the ordinary levitical singers, and that the description of the men as prophesying with a musical accompaniment involved more than that they played and sang in a peculiarly skilful manner. Not only were the men set apart to prophesy with a musical accompaniment, not to sing and play with a prophetic accompaniment, or in a prophetic, i.e. skilful manner, but also their three chiefs are called prophets or seers.[1] If the brief prayer which followed the list of Heman's sons formed part of the original it will offer a confirmation of this conclusion. For according to Rothstein's reconstruction the sentence ended with a petition that God would grant an abundance of visions. Such an ejaculation formed a fitting close to an account of the appointment of a body of men, whose function it was to prophesy in connexion with the cult. The men entrusted with this duty were made to pray for the divine furtherance in their specific task.

The section is part of the Chronicler's account, and links up directly with 23: 6a, according to which David divided the levites into courses. C did not enter into detail about this arrangement or, if he did, his account has been forced

---

[1] For the implication of this remarkable statement in its relation to the old Israelite cult I must be content to refer to my *Prophet and Priest in the Old Testament*, p. 130, note 2, and to add a reference to Dr. Johnson's valuable article in the *Expository Times*, 1936.

to give place to the account of the reviser. But after David had commanded the community to bring the ark into the temple, and to appoint its ministers, the levites, to conduct the cult there, he added a detail about that cult, which was to be entrusted to a select body from among the levitical singers. As he had done in his first order, so he did here: he took action on his own authority without advice from the leading priests, for according to C he was guided in all such matters by a divine revelation. When, again, C recognized the importance of prophecy and gave it a place in the regular cult, he showed a sense of the significance of that factor in the national religion. It may even be added that, when he spoke of the task being committed to a body of officials, he betrayed the extent to which prophecy had become canalized.

The question of the door-keepers is notoriously involved and perplexing, and it would be an abuse of the courtesy of the Schweich Trustees to attempt to enter on a general discussion. It is only in place to set down the contribution to the perplexity which appears in chap. 26. One general conclusion seems clear. The reviser, who distributed the priests, levites, and singers into their courses, has done the same here for the door-keepers in vv.1–19. He also included these officials among the levites, and derived them from the two families of Korah and Merari. He gave the names of the representatives of these two families, and was careful to provide the first-mentioned of the two, Meshelemyahu, with a levitical descent, while he stated that the second, Hosah, belonged to the Merarites.

But there are two sections of his account which at least suggest a different source. Thus Rothstein has drawn attention to the appearance of Obed-Edom between the two leaders of the Korahites and the Merarites, whose descendants are followed into the second generation, but who is himself provided with no levitical descent. These vv. 4–8 Rothstein therefore counted secondary. Again, certain features in vv. 13–19 point to a date soon after the Return and even to a particular situation during that period. The four entrances which are assigned to the temple,[1] the mysterious *parbar*, and the storehouse or בֵּית הָאֲסֻפִּים of v. 15[2] are all introduced as though they were so familiar that they needed no precise definition. The author also wrote about the gate of *Shalleketh* and the causeway beside it like one who was dealing with matters of common knowledge to every one in the Jerusalem of his time. He, further, it deserves to be noticed, had no hesitation in assigning to Obed-Edom the charge of one of the gates and in placing his descendants over a storehouse. In this he was in agreement with C who stated that Obed-Edom was entrusted with the treasures in the temple.[3]

To explain the intrusion of vv. 4-8, Rothstein suggested that the descendants of Obed-Edom, who is acknowledged to have been a foreigner in the early records, made good a claim to be admitted among the door-keepers at a period later than the time of the Return. The paragraph here, in his view, was added in order to include them among the levites. Yet the feature of the verses which drew Rothstein's attention was the absence of any levitical descent in the account of the men. Nor does this view pay sufficient attention to the statement in v. 15, where Obed-Edom appears among other levites in charge of one of the gates of the temple. Whether the section in which that remark occurs can be taken to refer to a specific period in the history of the temple or not, it is not later than the time of the Return.

In my judgement we are on safer ground when we count vv. 4-8 and vv. 14-18 older material which was incorporated into the later record, and which *may* derive from the Chronicler. That writer gave a position of honour to Obed-Edom because of his early association with the ark, though he made no effort to conceal that the man was not even of Israelite descent. He also dwelt, both here at v. 5 and at 13: 14, on the fact that God blessed him, as though

---

[1] Cf. I Chr. 9: 18, 24.   [2] Neh. 12: 25.
[3] Contrast II Chr. 25: 24 with II Kings 14: 14.

that was needed to explain the place he held. He recognized that not only was the man himself a door-keeper, but that one of his descendants reached a place of trust in the temple. But in the later period after the Return stricter views about the descent of the temple-servants came to prevail, as the vehement protest in Ezekiel proves. And the absence of Obed-Edom's name from the lists of I Chr. cc. 1-9 and from the book of Nehemiah suggests the opposite conclusion to that of Rothstein, viz. that the men were expelled from office rather than given a levitical descent. It may be necessary, however, to add that our knowledge of the conditions of the time, especially in connexion with the matter of the door-keepers, is so uncertain that any conclusion must be taken to be merely tentative. All that can be claimed is that there is ground for recognizing two alternatives on the subject.

The situation becomes much worse in the final verses of the chapter. The text is very bad: thus v. 23 cannot be translated as it stands, and 'the sons of Ladan, the sons of the Gershonites belonging to Ladan, the heads of the fathers' houses belonging to Ladan the Gershonite' in v. 21 looks more like three readings which have been combined by a copyist than anything else. The phraseology employed varies also in a way which is quite inexplicable. Within the five opening verses we read of treasuries of the house of the Lord, treasuries of the house of God, treasuries of the consecrated things, and treasuries *simpliciter*. It is equally hard to credit that there were four such sets of rooms, as that the same man varied his description without reason. The Hebronites of v. 30 had oversight of Israel on the western bank of the Jordan in connexion with מְלֶאכֶת יהוה or the business of the Lord, while their or his brethren fulfilled a similar task on the eastern bank and dealt with דְּבַר האלהים every matter pertaining to God, v. 32. It is scarcely likely that the same man used the variant phrases in what are practically consecutive sentences. Nor is it easy to see why the divine name varies at the beginning and the end of the passage. The references, again, to officers in charge of affairs in Reuben, Gad, and Manasseh, and the statement that some of the treasures were derived from war-spoils, won by Samuel and Saul and Abner and Joab, point to an early date for part of the material. The men of the Return, so far as we know, took no interest in the country on the east of Jordan and were not likely to credit Abner or Saul with any share in providing for the temple. The material appears to be a collection of *disjecta membra* which have been put together—they cannot be said to have been edited—and inserted at the end of a passage which referred to the similar subject of the temple treasuries.

The analysis which has been offered confirms the impression that the chapters which have been passed in review present the most perplexing riddle which meets a student of the Books of Chronicles. Those who have devoted most time and attention to their contents will most readily acknowledge the tentative character of any conclusions which they venture to present. It is clear, however, that there is evidence for several hands having contributed to the material, though opinion may justly vary as to the number of writers who can be recognized. It is not hard to understand why the passage received special attention, when we break finally from the attitude of the author of Ezra, and reject his view that all the arrangements as to the cult of the second temple and as to the officials who served that cult were settled with the advent of Joshua the high-priest and his fellow exiles. Any one who rejects that smooth solution will recognize that the infant community at Jerusalem was faced with grave difficulties in determining the lines of its future policy after the confusion which resulted from the Exile. There were real divergencies of opinion, which were also justifiable, as to the principles which ought to govern that policy. Naturally the men who held these convictions sought to support their attitude through an appeal to the past. Inevitably the men turned their attention to the story of the foundation of the first temple, and attempted to find support in the record of David's action, when he planned the first sanctuary. It becomes possible to recognize why an account of David's orders to Solomon on the subject was written, and why it betrays the presence of annotations and additions throughout. It also becomes possible to realize why there should appear the mention of questions such as the relation between the two lines of priests in 24: 1–6. The matter there dealt with is so wholly out of place in connexion with the situation under David that it betrays at once the period of the Return. It bears the marks of a writer who was putting a decision of his own time under the high authority of King David.

There is, however, another feature of the chapters in the form in which we possess them, which in my judgement is clear. It has all been revised by a writer who attempted to arrange the material in order to bring out the courses of the several classes of temple officials. He divided the priests, the levites, the singers whom he did not identify with the levites, and the door-keepers into twenty-four courses for each. To serve this end, he used older material, the source of which it is not always possible to determine, but he used what he thus borrowed for his particular purpose. Now the attitude of this reviser can be recognized in certain directions. His work is integrally related to the age of 20 years, assigned to the levites for their entry on office. It is also closely related to the paragraph which defined the relative status of levite and priest, and defined this after the terms of the late law. He therefore held the position represented in that paragraph and made the temple a surrogate for the tabernacle. Finally, he spoke of David as having consulted with the priests in any arrangement of the clerical courses. He even stated at one place that, in what he did about the clergy, David was obeying the command which God issued to Moses. In all these respects his account corresponds with that which has already been recognized in our preceding chapters.

It may be legitimate to conclude this discussion with a

suggestion as to the reason which produced the divergence between the 30 year and 20 year age-limit for the levites' entry on office. There was a period after the restoration of the second temple which was attended by a scarcity of these officials, for Ezra took measures to supply the deficiency, before he led his company of returned exiles back to Jerusalem. In another connexion I have pointed out that the story of Korah's rebellion may preserve the memory of a time when the levites, who had hitherto occupied a higher status, were relegated to the lower position which the later law assigned to them relatively to the priesthood. While some of their number accepted the situation, a contingent refused to submit, were excommunicated, and hived off to form the nucleus of the later Samaritan schism.[1] One result of this was to produce a serious scarcity in the number of levites who were available for the cult at Jerusalem. The authorities met the difficulty by lowering the age at which the levites were admitted to office.

[1] In *Post-Exilic Judaism*, p. 239 f. with note.

V

HEZEKIAH'S REFORM

THE importance which the Chronicler attached to the reform which Hezekiah effected after the apostasy under Ahaz appears from the extent of space he devoted to it in his history. No less than three chapters, II. 29–31, are occupied with the subject; and these have no parallel in Kings, but are peculiar to his account. Yet this fact, significant though it is, does not exhaust the evidence for C's interest in the matter. That can only be fully measured, when the two accounts of the reign are compared in some detail. For the later historian has practically recast the work of his predecessor with the result that he has made the reform dominate the reign, and has relegated the defeat of Sennacherib and the deliverance of Jerusalem into a relatively inferior position. The study of his method in this particular case throws light on the aims which guided him in all his work, and illustrates afresh the extent to which he was prepared to modify the facts of history in order to adapt them to his purpose.

K, then, began his story of the reign with high praise of Hezekiah's conduct in matters of religion; but he couched this in somewhat general terms, except that he singled out for special approbation the royal act in removing from the temple the serpent which Moses had made. He added that the king showed a peculiar trust in the God of Israel, and that the Lord was with him, giving him success in his military enterprises. The historian was clearly of opinion that the rebellion against Assyria and a war against the Philistines were inspired by the king's faith in the divine help and were successful, because that faith met its reward, II Kings 18: 2–8. He then related very briefly the campaign of Shalmaneser, which resulted in the ruin of Samaria and the captivity of northern Israel. These events he dated during the fourth to the sixth years of the reign of the Judean king. The rest of his account is occupied with the story of the campaign of Sennacherib, which he dated in the fourteenth year of Hezekiah, and which was followed by the embassy from Babylon with its attendant miracle.

On the other hand, C entered at great detail into the measures of reform which were carried out by the king. How necessary these were he suggested by insisting, much more than K had done, on the gravity of the defection under Ahaz. According to him that king had shut up the temple, had destroyed the sacrificial vessels, and had built altars to heathen gods in the streets of the capital. The national religion had practically been in abeyance during the reign. Accordingly, as the need for reform was greater, its scope was much wider than anything which appeared in K. For, while Hezekiah devoted special attention to the purification of the temple, the community under his influence removed the foreign altars which defiled Jerusalem, and even went so far as to purge the whole land of every heathen emblem. C, however, supplied no dates for the successive stages of this reform, except that he stated, as a proof of the pious zeal of the young king, that Hezekiah began it in the first month of the first year of his reign. When he came to describe its second stage, the celebration of passover at the temple, he left his readers to infer that it must have taken place after the fall of Samaria, since the king took steps to secure the presence of Israelites at the rite; but the exact date did not interest the historian. In the same way, when he related the campaign of Sennacherib, he ignored the date which K had supplied. What to him was of much greater significance was that it took place 'after these things and after this faithfulness', 32: 1. He underlined the religious lesson which K had only suggested; the marvellous deliverance of Judah was the direct outcome of its king's faithfulness in restoring his kingdom to allegiance and dependence on its God. Thus, in contrast with K, who made the defeat of Assyria the leading feature of the reign, C made the rededication of the temple and the passover celebration dominate everything else.

The same interest appears in his story of the campaign. His account can be paralleled with a series of extracts from his predecessor,[1] but the whole is given a new aspect through a change of emphasis. Since the marvellous deliverance was directly due to Hezekiah's piety, the king must have relied absolutely on the help of God. Therefore C omitted from the message of the Assyrian king any reference to Judah's hope of aid from Egypt, K. 18: 21, 24. Where K wrote about the fear which drove the Judean king to prayer, C made him have recourse to God in faith, 32: 6–8. In the same way he ignored the request of the royal officers that the Rabshakeh should not speak to the Jewish population in their own language: there was no panic in the capital, because king and people were relying on the divine help. Again, because the marvellous and complete character of the divine deliverance was heightened, the disastrous condition to which Sennacherib reduced the kingdom was minimized. There is no mention of the fact that the provincial towns were captured and that many of their inhabitants were carried into captivity. Instead of this, it is stated that the invader encamped against these towns and intended to break them up, v. 1. The reader does not receive the impression, so vividly conveyed in K, that Jerusalem was the one remaining centre of resistance and that Hezekiah was shut up in his capital like a bird in a cage. The letter of the Assyrian king was reported, but nothing was said about the humiliating demands which it contained, or about the extent to which Hezekiah complied with these demands. The letter in C's report contained merely a series of insults directed against the God of Israel and against Hezekiah, His servant. As such, it formed another reason for Sennacherib's complete and ignominious overthrow.

In the account of Hezekiah's sickness, of the resultant miracle and of the embassy from Babylonia, it is equally

[1] Cf. II Kings 18: 13, 17, 19, 22, 29–35; 19: 1 f., 35–37; 20: 1.

significant to notice that C, without entirely omitting these events, slurred them over. Thus at v. 24b he reduced K. 20: 1b–11 to a curt sentence: Hezekiah prayed unto the Lord, and He spake unto him and gave him a sign. At v. 25 he dealt in the same way with K. 20: 12–19, and was content to say that the king did not show due gratitude for the sign which was granted in answer to his prayer. There, however, he omitted all reference to the embassy from Babylonia; and, when he did refer to that embassy in v. 31, he wrote as though its only purpose had been to inquire into the miracle. Yet he practically acknowledged that another purpose had been behind it, since he went on to say that, in connexion with it, God left Hezekiah to his own devices in order to know what was in his heart. But he softened the condemnation which was implicit in this remark, since he continued that Hezekiah and Jerusalem repented of their conduct, and that, because of this repentance, the divine wrath did not fall upon the city during the king's lifetime.

The Chronicler was dominated throughout by more than a desire to present Hezekiah as the faithful successor of David who restored the religion of his nation after the lapse under Ahaz, and who in his work of reform gave special attention to the temple and its cult. He was also presenting the conception of the true policy of a wise and devout king of the little state, which has already appeared in the study of his attitude to prophecy. Such a king must rely absolutely on the power of religion to give character to a nation, and even to maintain its independence. Hezekiah's faith had been triumphantly vindicated at the beginning of his reign in the collapse of Sennacherib, and, when he failed to maintain it at a later date, his repentant return to the true attitude prevented Judah from following Samaria into ruin. That method of writing history has its undoubted drawbacks, but it has also a perennial fascination for the minds of men. We have our modern school of historians who are able to trace all the course of man's wild and gallant efforts through the centuries to its simple source in economic necessity. But the preoccupation with which such historians start has always led them to select from the tangled web of the past the facts which support their judgement and to pass lightly over the rest. It has been possible to trace the Chronicler, as he used his material to present his thesis, or to teach his lesson. The pet thesis of a modern historian and the moral passion of a pious historian are not unlike each other in their sources and in their methods.

The chapters which describe Hezekiah's reform have naturally received a great deal of attention. Earlier scholars, such as Kittel, were peculiarly interested in the question as to the amount of confidence which could be placed in the document as a historical record of events. They discussed very fully the relation between the reform under Josiah and that assigned to Hezekiah from this point of view. It may be said that the older verdict inclined strongly to the opinion that the record of the earlier reform-movement must be received with extreme scepticism, and that, while there was a recoil during Hezekiah's reign against the laxity which prevailed under Ahaz, the account in Chronicles has been so coloured by elements taken from the greater movement in Josiah's reign, as to be practically of little historical value. The line of inquiry which is followed in this study does not permit any detailed reference to the purely historical debate. But it may be legitimate to direct attention here to one aspect of the subject. The somewhat undue absorption in the historical questions which gather round these chapters has had a certain mischievous result in two directions. On the one hand, it has led many scholars to emphasize to a quite undue extent the resemblances between the accounts of the two reforms. It was an inevitable outcome of their belief that the earlier movement was largely a reproduction of the later that they set in high relief every correspondence between the two, with the result that the equally significant differences dropped into the background. Yet, however we are to explain these differences, they are there, and they are of sufficient gravity to constitute a real factor in a perplexing question. From the point of view of one who is chiefly interested in the Chronicler's attitude they are even of peculiar importance. Another result of this line of approach to the subject has been that students have unconsciously placed undue confidence in the historical accuracy of the story of Josiah's reform. It has become usual to approach the earlier three chapters in Chronicles with hesitation over every detail, and to accept the later record with entire confidence. Yet, to go no further into detail, the close resemblance between certain elements of that record in Kings and Chronicles leaves on a reader the suspicion that the two accounts have been brought into harmony, and that the story of Josiah's reform has received a revision.

The three chapters, then, since they derived originally from C and are peculiar to him, present his view of the situation; and, whatever sources of information he employed, are adapted to show what in his judgement was the conduct which befitted a reforming king. The account proceeded along a series of well-marked stages. It began with the purification of the temple, which was carried out with scrupulous care, 29: 3–19. This was followed by a *hanukkah*, the rededication of the purified sanctuary, vv. 20–30, and this in turn by the resumption of the sacrificial worship on the part of the people, vv. 31–6. The next stage was the celebration of passover at the temple, when for the first time that rite was transferred from the homes of the people to the sanctuary at Jerusalem. The feature in it, on which C laid most stress, was the fact that Hezekiah showed himself anxious to secure the presence of representatives from northern Israel, 30: 1–20. Passover was followed by the festival of unleavened bread, in which also men from Israel took part. On this occasion the festival was continued for fourteen days, vv. 21–7. Thereafter the king took steps to purify the land of Israel from every heathen emblem, 31: 1. Finally, Hezekiah appointed the courses of the temple-clergy, and made a series of regulations to provide for their support. He also arranged for rooms about the temple in which the offerings were to be stored, and for officials to supervise these stores and to distribute their contents, chap. 31: 2–21. It will be necessary to examine in some detail each of the stages in this reform.

In his account of the purification of the temple, C made Hezekiah gather the priests and levites into a plaza before the sanctuary in order to receive their instructions, 29: 4. The king, however, when he bade the men sanctify themselves for the duty, only addressed the levites, v. 5; and it was representatives of those clergy, chosen from certain levitical tribes, who carried out the task, vv. 12 ff., and, who, after it was completed, reported the fact to their master, vv. 18 f. The initiative here was taken by the king without consultation with the priests, as it was when David gave directions about the transference of the ark, I. 15: 11, and when he issued his final orders about the future temple, I. 23: 2–6a and 25: 1.

Büchler drew attention to the anomalous feature here that, while both priests and levites were summoned to receive their instructions, only the levites were addressed on the subject of the purification. He was of opinion that in the original version the gathering was confined to the priests, and that the levites were added later.[1] In order to explain why, though Hezekiah only convened the priests, he addressed them as levites, he made the suggestion that in v. 5 levites means both priests and levites. In support of this suggestion, he could appeal to only one passage in II. 30: 27, where it is stated that 'the priests the levites arose and blessed the people'. But this verse offers two readings: M.T. and LXX^B, which were followed by the R.V., read 'the levitical priests', some Hebrew MSS. and LXX^A have 'the priests and the levites'. Neither reading offers any support to Büchler's view that the priests were

---

[1] *Z.A.W*, 1899, pp. 109 ff. In his view the purpose of the addition was to give the levites a higher status through insistence on their services in connexion with the musical side of the cult.

described *as* levites. Nor has he felt it necessary to explain why the original Chronicler, after saying that Hezekiah convened the priests, made him suddenly change his form of address, and give the men what, even on Büchler's explanation, was so unusual a title.

Further, Büchler has ignored that the men who obeyed the royal instructions were representative members of certain levitical clans, and therefore undoubted levites. Kittel, who holds that the instructions were issued to both priests and levites under the general title of levites, is met by the difficulty of explaining v. 11. There, Hezekiah is made to close his instructions to the men by exhorting them to diligence, because the Lord had chosen them to stand before Him, to minister unto Him, and that they should be His ministers and burn incense. How can such a description of the functions exercised by the men be made applicable to both priests and levites? Kittel sought to meet the difficulty by the statement that שֵׁרֵת to minister was employed in a double sense. It was first used in a general sense which covered the duties of both bodies of the clergy, so that the two orders were chosen to stand before the Lord to minister to Him. It was afterwards used with a reference to the distinctive tasks of the two: the levites were to act as divine ministers, while the priests alone had the right to burn incense. Yet, even if it were legitimate to suppose that the same word was used within a single sentence in a double sense, the proposed explanation does not remove the difficulty. For presumably the first clause described both priest and levite as standing before the Lord and ministering unto Him. Now this is the dignity which the law denied to the levite and reserved to the priest. In it the priests stood before the Lord and ministered to Him, the levites stood before the priests and ministered to them. On Kittel's presuppositions this was anomalous.

The only method which can reduce the passage to order is to recognize that a later hand introduced the priests at v. 4, and assigned to them the privilege and duty of entering

the most holy place for the purpose of purifying it at v. 16.
The latter verse betrays itself as an intrusion, since it breaks
the close connexion between vv. 15 and 17. But there is
another indication of the hand of the reviser at the close
of v. 15, where it is stated that the levites, whose names had
been given, went in to cleanse the temple according to the
royal orders בְּדִבְרֵי יהוה by the words of the Lord. The last
two Hebrew words have no force in a narrative which made
the reform movement take its initiative in the decree of
Hezekiah and made him issue instructions to the clergy.
They are another addition by the reviser who stated that
the purification of the temple, though due to the king's
order, was carried out in strict conformity with the Mosaic
law, which forbade the levites to enter the holy of holies.
When these additions are removed, the text agrees with the
attitude of the original Chronicler.

After the temple had been purged of every heathen
emblem, the way was clear for the next stage, the rededication of the sanctuary and the altar, which follows in vv. 20–
30. Here Kittel has drawn attention to the peculiarity of
v. 25 in its present connexion, since there Hezekiah is said
to have appointed certain levites to conduct a musical
service as an accompaniment to dedication sacrifices which,
according to vv. 22–4, had already been offered. He also
remarked on the express statement that in his action on the
occasion the king conformed to the directions of David who
was guided in the matter by prophets. Accordingly, Kittel
and Benzinger pronounced the verse to be a late addition,
which was inserted in order to advance the status of the
levites by dwelling on their functions as musicians. But
the two scholars failed to recognize that merely to cut out
the verse does not meet the real difficulty of the passage.
The fact remains that the sacrifices which had already been
offered in connexion with the service of rededication are
here resumed, and, even if we omit the statement that
Hezekiah appointed certain levites to supply a musical
accompaniment, emphasis is laid on that accompaniment

in v. 26. As soon as this repetition of the sacrificial acts is
recognized, other differences between vv. 20–4 and vv. 25–
30 become apparent. In the former passage the sacrifices
were entirely in the hands of the priests, the sons of Aaron,
with no mention of any participation on the part of the
levites: in the later passage the priests do not appear at
all. Again, in the earlier passage, emphasis is laid on the
atoning character of the sacrifices; seven he-goats were set
apart for this purpose by the imposition of the hands of king
and congregation, and the king commanded that both
burnt-offering and sin-offering should be made for all
Israel. In the later passage the sacrifice consisted of burnt-
offerings without mention of any sin-offerings.

It is of interest to compare the account here with the
parallel description of two similar services. The first is the
service of dedication after Solomon had completed the
temple in II. 5: 2–14, 7: 1 ff. There also the sacrifices were
duplicated:[1] in the one case they were offered before the
ark, and there is no mention of any priests having taken part
in the ritual, in the other they were offered by the priests
on the altar and were accepted by the descent of the divine
fire. In neither case was there any mention of sin-offerings.
The other occasion was that of the dedication of the second
temple, Ezra 6: 16–18. There the officiants were the priests
with their attendant levites, and the sacrifices included
twelve he-goats for a sin-offering for all Israel. Thereafter
the priests were set in their divisions and the levites in their
courses for the service of God, as it is written in the book of
Moses. The duplication here and at Solomon's dedication
is enough to prove the presence of two hands. Here, as at
II. 5: 2 ff, the Chronicler in vv. 25–30 made the sacrifices
consist of burnt-offerings, and did not specify the officiants
at the altar. Instead he dwelt on the fact that Hezekiah
began the ritual by the appointment of levitical singers
according to the commandment of David and certain
prophets. These were the men whom, according to C in

[1] Cf. the analysis at pp. 37 ff.

I. 25: 1–6, David set apart to prophesy with a musical accompaniment at the temple-cult, so that the ritual included a liturgy which made its purpose and meaning clear. The reviser, who added vv. 21–4, had a double end to serve. He put the priests into their rightful place as conducting the sacrifices: but he also made the dedication of the temple conform to the ritual of the men of the Return and emphasized the element of atonement in it.[1]

When the sanctuary and altar had been reconsecrated, the ordinary sacrificial worship was resumed at the temple, vv. 31–6. In his account of the purification and dedication, C had dwelt on the part taken by the levites and had not confined their functions to the choral service. It is natural, therefore, to find that, when the resumption of the customary sacrifices was described, the levites were said to have been more upright in heart to sanctify themselves than the priests v. 34. The expression, as Kittel recognized, casts a certain slur on the priests. Yet it is not easy to find any justification for that slur in the text as it stands at present, since in it the

---

[1] There is a minor point here, which may deserve at least a note. When he dealt with v. 22, Kittel appears to have believed that the priests slew the victims which were destined for ordinary burnt-offerings, and contrasted the practice of lay-slaughter in Lev. 1: 5 f., 11 as well as the fact that in Ezek. 44: 11 this duty was assigned to the levites. He, therefore, concluded that in this respect the method of sacrifice did not conform to the later law. But his statement on the subject is not quite accurate. The text, when it described the slaughter of the victims for burnt-offerings, made use of the ambiguous 'they slew', which does not necessarily imply that the priests performed the act. In connexion with the manipulation of the blood of these victims, however, it is definitely stated that this was done by the priests. Also, when the victims were the he-goats destined for the sin-offerings, the language is more precise. In v. 24, after the king and congregation had laid their hands on these goats, the priests both slew them and manipulated their blood. Hänel has devoted special attention to the passage in his 'Das Recht der Schlachtung in der chronistischen Literatur', *Z.A.W.* 1937, p. 46: but in my judgement his conclusions are vitiated by his failure to recognize that there is a duplication of the ceremony in the passage. He has attempted to treat it as a unity.

priests occupied the most important position, and showed
no reluctance to appear at Hezekiah's summons or to fulfil
his commands. On the other hand, when it has been
recognized that the text has been revised in the interests of
these priests, it becomes clear that such a slur upon them,
if it was intended, was quite in keeping with the attitude
of the original narrative.

After this appears the account of the measures Hezekiah
undertook for a celebration of passover at the temple,
30: 1–12, which was followed by a purification of Jerusalem
from all heathen emblems, v. 14, and associated with the
festival of unleavened bread. Here C's account of Hezekiah's reform comes into closer relation to the story of the
reform under Josiah. This is not the place to enter into a
full discussion of the perplexing questions which arise on
that subject, since any such discussion must cover a wider
field than is germane to the present study. But it is in place
to direct attention to the remarkable divergence in these
two passovers, as they are described by C.

It will then be agreed that two questions in connexion
with this celebration of passover, whether it took place
under both kings or only under Josiah, continue to engage
the attention of students. The first of these is that we have
here the first *historical* mention of passover having taken
place at a sanctuary, with priests in attendance, instead of
the family rite described in Exod. 12: 1–14, where neither
sanctuary nor priest was essential to its validity. The other
involves the attempt to determine the relation of this new
feature of the ritual to the book of the law which was discovered in the temple when Josiah repaired it, with all the
conclusions which have been based on the reality of this
relation.

Now the outstanding feature in C's account of Hezekiah's
passover is that he gave no attention to either of these
questions. His leading interest in the event from beginning
to end was that the whole nation, Judah and Israel, took
part in the ceremonial at the temple. He described the

measures which the king took in order to invite the remanent
Israelites to a share in the rite. He entered into some detail
as to the comparative failure which attended the efforts to
unite the nation, and told how representatives of parts of
Israel accepted the invitation. In order to make the presence
of these men possible, Judah was prepared to postpone not
only passover but the following festival of unleavened bread
into the second month. Because the northern visitors were
ceremonially unclean, measures were taken to guarantee
their ritual purity; and, because these measures were not
entirely effective, the king himself prayed for the divine
forgiveness of a breach of the law in the case of some of the
worshippers. It was natural, therefore, that, when he
described Josiah's passover, he was content to state that the
children of Israel who were present kept the passover at that
time with its attendant festival, 35: 17 f. In the connexion
in which he had placed the two events it was unnecessary
to say more, because Hezekiah's conduct had made it clear
that Israel had its place in the national celebration.

On the other hand, in his account of Josiah's passover,
C entered into considerable detail as to the method in which
the rite was celebrated, chap. 35. That, again, was natural,
when it is recognized that the method of celebration was a
novelty. When passover ceased to be a family rite, and was
transferred from the home to the sanctuary, some change
in its form was inevitable: and C, with his interest in everything which concerned the cult, was not likely to lose the
opportunity of sketching the use which was then instituted.
The later chapter has a direct bearing on the first of our
questions, that of the transference of passover from the
home to the sanctuary.

One final feature in C's account of the two reforms cannot
be ignored here. In neither case did he associate the royal
action with the book of the law which Josiah discovered in
the temple. His description of Josiah's passover is isolated
and contains no hint of its having been the outcome of that
momentous discovery; and, obviously, nothing can prove

more clearly his sense of the independence of the two events than that he dated Hezekiah's movement long before the book was found. All who are convinced that Josiah was the first who, in the interests of centralization, transferred passover to the sanctuary, that Deuteronomy was the discovered book on which the reform was based, and that it had been revised in the interests of centralization, must take more seriously the evidence of this chapter in Chronicles. It makes no real difference here, though the historical value of C's story of Hezekiah's reform is seriously impugned. The fact remains that a responsible writer, whose book has found its way into the Jewish Canon, had no hesitation in dating the first tentative movement for centralization, and the change of locus for passover in the time of Hezekiah, and that, by doing this, he made it impossible to connect either movement with the discovery of the book of the law. The later his account is placed, the more difficult does it become to see the motive which impelled him to take this attitude.[1]

[1] I may be forgiven for introducing here a personal explanation. Recently, in a review of one of my books, Dr. T. H. Robinson informed his readers that I did not accept the view that Josiah made the temple the sole centre for sacrificial worship; and, when the statement was challenged, added that others shared his opinion. I have never questioned that Josiah succeeded in centralizing sacrifice at Jerusalem: what I cannot accept is the generally received judgement that this movement was the outcome of the book found in the temple, and that this book was the Deuteronomic Code, which had been revised in order to adapt it as a basis for this far-reaching change in Jewish worship. It may be that I am partly guilty of having failed to make my meaning plain, and that this failure may be due to my silence about the mysterious book, its contents, and its source. The reason for this silence is the very simple one that I cannot pretend to know. One of the few facts which we do know about it is that it was submitted to a prophetess, and that she declared that no reform based on it would avail to prevent the doom which was impending over Jerusalem. It is difficult to reconcile this recorded utterance with the view that Josiah proceeded with a reform which was based on the book, and that this reform was so successful as to help Judah to recover from the destruction of the doomed city.

The Chronicler combined with his account of Hezekiah's passover a celebration of the festival of unleavened bread, in which also the northern Israelites took part, 30: 13–27. Two points deserve attention here.

The first is that there is some confusion in the text. Kittel thought that the passage again brought proof of a departure from the practice of lay-slaughter at passover. His reason was the statement in v. 15b that the priests and the levites were ashamed and sanctified themselves and brought burnt-offerings to the temple. He naturally concluded that these officials were the men who had killed the paschal victims in v. 15a. But he overlooked two facts when he drew this conclusion. On the one hand, the burnt-offerings which were brought into the temple cannot have been the paschal victims, since these were never consumed on the altar, but were eaten by the worshippers. Nor is there mention in any ritual law of such sacrifices in connexion with passover, though they were prescribed for the successive days of the festival of unleavened bread. On the other hand, when the levites are said in v. 17 to have slain the paschal victims, a special reason is given for their action. They only slew the victims for such worshippers as were not ceremonially clean, which implies that it was their condition of impurity which prevented the men from doing this for themselves.[1] It is necessary to rearrange the verses in order to bring them into order. If we read vv. 13, 14, 15b, 16 along with vv. 21 ff., we have a description of the festival of unleavened bread. The community at Jerusalem kept that feast in the second month, and used the opportunity to purge the city of all heathen emblems, as the king had purified the temple, vv. 13 f. The northern Israelites, who had come to Jerusalem for passover, took part in the following festival, v. 21. When we read in the same way vv. 12, 15a, 17–20 consecutively, it can be recognized that these in turn refer to passover. All

---

[1] Hänel in his reference to the passage in his article, 'Das Recht der Schlachtung', *Z.A.W.* 1937, p. 49, has also failed to notice that these burnt-offerings cannot have been the paschal victims.

Judah heartily accepted the royal proposal for transferring the rite to the temple, and they slew the victims on the fourteenth day of the second month. But, because in consequence of the novel situation many of the worshippers were ritually unclean, the levites killed the victims for these men. Some of the Israelites, however, were not in such a condition of purity as justified even their approach to the sanctuary, and for them Hezekiah offered intercessory prayer.

When we turn to the description of the festival of unleavened bread, one feature in the account is the diversity in the language used about the officiating clergy. The priests and the levites sanctified themselves and brought burnt-offerings into the temple, vv. 15 f.: the levites and the priests praised the Lord day by day, v. 21: Hezekiah commended all the levites who were well skilled, v. 22: a great number of the priests sanctified themselves, v. 24: the priests and the levites united with the community in thanksgiving, v. 25: the levitical priests[1] arose and blessed the people, v. 27.

This can hardly be original, but it is easier to recognize the abnormal character of the passage than to discover a sure method of correcting it. Kittel proposed to omit the levites in v. 15 on the ground that there both priests and levites incurred censure, whereas only the priests were blamed at v. 3. This is possible, and would be more so, if one were convinced that the earlier verse implied blame on the men. Besides, if the motive of the insertion had been to avoid the appearance of making the higher clergy the only delinquents, it would have been more natural to make the insertion when the matter was first mentioned. Nor does the omission of the levites from the verse suit the following statement in v. 16, which bears the mark of a reviser. He noted that, when it was said that priests and levites brought burnt-offerings into the temple, this was capable of implying

---

[1] So M.T. and LXX[B]: several MSS. and LXX[A] add a word and read 'the priests and the levites'.

an equal status for the two classes of the clergy. Accordingly he added that everything was carried out in strict accordance with the use of Jerusalem. The king's order might be allowed for once to change the date of the festival, in spite of the hesitation of his clergy, but in the actual administration of the ritual the law of Moses prevailed in its integrity. In v. 21, again, the priests have been intruded, for not only is the order of the words, levites and priests, unexampled, but there is no other instance of a desire to credit the priests with a share in the musical part of the ordinary service. The motive which prompted the reviser may have been to take off the edge from the special commendation which Hezekiah bestowed on the levites for their share in the ceremony.

Thus C gave the levites the leading position in his description of Hezekiah's passover. So far as the priests were concerned he confined himself to the statement that they showed a certain reluctance to take any part in it. On the other hand he credited the priests with a leading position in the festival of unleavened bread; they were prominent in connexion with the burnt-offerings which formed an element in the ceremony. But he recorded the hearty commendation which the king gave the levites because of the support they had given him throughout; and he gave them an equal place with the priests in the benediction of the people with which the rite closed. The latter statement remains true, whatever reading be adopted in v. 27. Even if we read the priests and the levites the verse implies that the levites shared in a privilege which was later reserved to the priests.

When the festival was over the holy land was purged of its idolatrous emblems; the Israelites who were found in the Judean towns went out to Judah and Benjamin, in Ephraim also and Manasseh, until they had destroyed them all, 31: 1.

The concluding section, 31: 2–19, details the arrangements Hezekiah made in connexion with the provision for the sacrificial worship at the temple. He distributed the officiating clergy into their courses, determined the source of the regular communal offerings, and in particular made regulations to guarantee a sufficient income for the priests and levites. The passage is very confused in its arrangement and uncertain in its terms, since it contains references to charges on the religious community the exact sense of which is far from clear. Hence any conclusions which are presented must be recognized as tentative in their character.

The opening verse states that the king divided the priests and levites into their courses, but defines the respective duties of the two bodies in an unusual way: their service was for burnt-offerings and for peace-offerings to minister and to give thanks and to praise in the gates of the camp of the Lord. Büchler proposed to omit 'and to give thanks and to praise' as a later addition.[1] The proposal seems violent, since the words appear in the versions and are natural in any reference to the functions of the levites. Indeed they may be said to be necessary here, since, if they are omitted, there is left nothing except 'to serve in the gates', which would limit the levites to acting as door-keepers. The curious expression, the gates of the camp of the Lord, appears again at I. 9: 18 ff.; but to expect light from that quarter is to look for light in a deeper darkness. One hint may come from the last clause in the passage, where the men who were over the camp of the Lord are equated with the keepers of the entry or door-keepers. In that case our verse may describe the levites as musicians and door-keepers, so that they were confined to the humble duties about the sanctuary. There is, it may be noted, no mention that Hezekiah, in making these arrangements, restored the conditions which had been introduced by David. The king also made provision that the charges for the morning and evening *tamidh* and for the major and minor festivals should be defrayed from the royal exchequer. The sacrifices mentioned here appear in full detail in Num. chaps. 28 f., and

[1] Kittel entered the reading in *B.H.*, but added a query.

the writer probably referred to that table of offerings when he wrote about the law of the Lord.

The next section, vv. 4–16, is devoted to Hezekiah's measures for the provision of adequate resources for the temple clergy, and is extremely confused in its terms. It closes, however, with three verses, 17–19, which offer a summary of those provisions and which ought to be marked as such by being separated from what precedes them. The verses open with ואת, which the R.V. understood to be the sign of accusative. It has therefore made vv. 16 and 17 continuous. But the noun which follows ואת is not dependent on or governed by any preceding verb. The word is an instance of the late usage which emphasized a new subject by prefixing את: and might be translated: as regards, or so far as concerns their register.[1] The verse begins a summing-up and states that the register of the priests for their duties was by genealogy, while the duties of the levites began from the age of 20 years. The purpose of this register is given in v. 18: it was to guarantee that the wives and children of the officiating priests had a sufficient provision. Verse 19 continued the same subject by saying that men were appointed to see that the families of the priests who were not serving on the rota were duly supplied, and to make provision for the levites. The verses are thus closely connected and offer a summary of the arrangements made to meet the needs of the temple-clergy. Three things are noteworthy in their terms. They ignored entirely the earlier appointment of a commission of levites and of Korah and his associates, though these were in charge of a similar task. They further dealt in cursory fashion with the needs of the levites, as compared with those of the priests. They are also later than the work of the Chronicler, since they

---

[1] Kittel reached the same conclusion by reading וזאת, in which reading he followed the LXX. It is more probable that the translators made the change in the text, because a literal translation would not have made the sense clear to their Greek readers. For the late usage of ואת cf. *B.D.B.* את 3.

made the levites enter on office at 20 years of age.[1] I suggest that they may be combined with vv. 2 f., where again
we find a reference, not to arrangements made by David,
but to the later law, and that they present a summary of
Hezekiah's dealings with the cult and its ministers. The
king distributed the priests and levites in their courses,
assigning to each class its separate tasks. He made provision
for the cost of the communal sacrifices, and he made
arrangements for the maintenance of the temple-clergy.
What remains was earlier material.

According to that earlier material, vv. 4-16, Hezekiah
ordered the people to give the portion of the priests and
levites in order that they might devote themselves to the law
of the Lord.[2] The king did not lay down a new regulation
on the subject, but merely enforced the observance of one
which already existed, for we find the people responding as
though they knew what was required of them. The details
of the way in which the order was carried into effect appear
in their response, not in the original ordinance. Kittel has
suggested that the new arrangements were made to prevent
the clergy from deserting the temple and falling away to the
high places. But that cannot well have been the sense of
the writer here, since he has immediately before described the
destruction of the local sanctuaries, so that the temptation
to resort to them was non-existent. Bertheau was of opinion
that the aim was to prevent the men from having recourse
to other means of livelihood, and this judgement is more
probable, especially if we combine with it the view that the
passage reflects conditions which prevailed before and after
the Return. For we find at least two indications of measures
having been adopted then to meet similar difficulties. Thus
it is said that at some period, because they did not receive
such provision, the levites and singers had fled, every one
to his field, Neh. 13: 10. Again, the religious community,
according to the pact of Neh. c. 10, found it necessary to

---

[1] Cf. p. 81.
[2] LXX reads: τῇ λειτουργίᾳ οἴκου Κυρίου.

take measures to guarantee that the offerings which were
devoted to the support of the priests and levites reached the
temple. There also the offerings were no novelty. The position of affairs under the pact resembles that which appears
here. So long as the kingdom existed the king was responsible for the communal offerings; when it ceased, the
community must meet those charges, and met it by a poll
tax. But the faithful were always responsible for meeting
the needs of the clergy: all that was needed there was to
guarantee that their offerings reached their destination.

In the description of the response made by the community to the royal command there is some confusion.
To begin with the minor and easier question, 'the tithe of
consecrated things' in v. 6 cannot be correct, since these were
dedicated in their entirety. We must omit the tithe.[1] The
crux is in the beginning of the verse. It had already been
stated that the children of Israel brought in abundantly the
first-fruits of corn, wine, oil, and honey, and also the tithe of
all things, and to this v. 6 adds 'and the children of Israel
and Judah who lived in the towns of Judah, they also, or,
even they, brought in the tithe of oxen and sheep'. Evidently
this cattle-tithe was additional to the tithe of all things. Since
the children of Israel who lived in the Judean towns is C's
usual description of those Israelites who transferred themselves to Judah after Jeroboam's apostasy,[2] it would be
natural to conclude that the men took on the obligation of
the country of their adoption, and paid a second tithe. But
the mention of Judah is puzzling, as there was no reason for
stating that the Judeans lived in their own towns. The
LXX carried back 'the children of Israel and Judah'
into the preceding verse, and made these the men who
brought in the tithes of all things. It then read in v. 6: those
who were living in the Judean towns, even they, brought
in the cattle-tithes. But these men in the Judean towns can
only be the refugee Israelites, and it cannot be supposed

---

[1] With Kittel, *B.H.*
[2] Cf. II. 10: 17, 11: 16, 30: 25.

that they alone paid the second tithe. Yet the translators did recognize that there was a distinction here between the contributions from north and south Israel.[1] The simplest solution is to transfer ויהודה or ובני יהודה to the beginning of v. 6, and read: Judah, or, the children of Judah, and the refugee Israelites, they also, or, even they, paid the cattle-tithe. This not only brings together the familiar description of those refugee Israelites, but it explains why these men are specially said to have paid this tithe. They followed the practice of their new country, and in this respect differed from their brethren of v. 5.

Now the first-fruits which the children of Israel brought correspond with the Deuteronomic law, except that Deut. 18:4, in commanding these to be given to the levites, included wool and omitted דְּבַשׁ or honey; the increase of the field is also a common expression in Deuteronomy. On the other hand, a law which prescribed a tithe of cattle and sheep only appears in Lev. 27: 32 f., although the specific destination of this offering is not defined—it is merely said to be holy unto the Lord. What precisely is meant by the tithe of all things in v. 5 is not certain, but from its connexion with what precedes and from its contrast with the following cattle-tithe this was probably a tithe on cereals. As such it agrees with the tithe which appears in Deuteronomy; but it disagrees with that law in the purpose to which the tithe was devoted. According to the law it was employed during two years in furnishing a communal meal at the sanctuary in which the levite shared, in the third year it provided a feast in which the levites and the poor had a share, Deut. 14: 22–9. Thus the cereal tithe is a prominent feature of the Deuteronomic Code and was there partly devoted to the

---

[1] Benzinger simply cut out וִיהוּדָה, though he offered no reason for its appearance in both our texts. But this compelled him to give a double sense to 'the children of Israel' in two consecutive verses, since he took the expression to mean Judeans in v. 5 and refugee Israelites in v. 6. It also made the refugee Israelites the only men who were said to have paid the cattle-tithe, and failed to explain the double tithe.

support of the levites, while the cattle-tithe appears only in Leviticus, where its destination is not specifically defined. The provenance of these two laws is, in my judgement, from Israel and Judah respectively. I suggest that at some period during the Exile or after the Return these offerings were devoted to the purpose of the maintenance of the clergy, because their needs were pressing at the time, and that the Chronicler carried back the regulation to Hezekiah, whom he made the pattern reformer among the early kings.

When we turn to the constituents of the heaps into which the offerings were gathered, we find Azariah the high-priest informing Hezekiah that the supply had been more than sufficient and employing the general term הַתְּרוּמָה the oblations, v. 10. When the heaps were transferred to the chambers prepared for them, they appear as oblations, tithes, and dedicated things, v. 12. Now according to Num. 18: 8–11 the oblation was the specific provision for the priests, in contrast with the tithe for the levites, vv. 21 ff. Again, because Nehemiah found that the portions allotted to the levites had not been given to them, he issued orders which resulted in the cereal tithe being brought to the treasuries, Neh. 13: 10–12. He also referred to a chamber in which had formerly been stored the cereal tithes given by commandment to the levites, while the oblations were for the priests, 13: 4. He further mentioned chambers for the oblations, the first-fruits, and the tithes to gather into them the portions appointed in the law for the priests and levites. Throughout, these passages agree with the regulations which Hezekiah was said to have laid down and with the terms of the pact of Neh. c. 10. They all agree that the cereal tithes were destined for the levites. Even the latest law did not contradict this, for it ordered that the oblations and the fat of oil, vintage, and corn, their first-fruits, belong to the priests, while the tithe goes to the levites, except a tithe of that tithe, which was paid over to the priests, Num. 18: 11 ff., 26, 28.

The resemblances between our passage and the regulations made on the same subject in the book of Nehemiah
and in the later law justify the inference that we have here
a reflection of the conditions which emerged about the
period of the Return. At that period it was obviously
necessary to make provision for the temple-clergy, if the
sacrificial worship was to continue. It is also clear that the
new arrangements must have involved an adjustment of
the older law in order to adapt it to the new conditions. On
the one hand, the centralization of the sacrificial worship
brought about an increase in the number of the temple-
clergy, who were entirely dependent on the gifts of the
faithful. On the other hand, men from both the old kingdoms combined under Josiah to maintain the common
worship. Their divergent practices needed to be reconciled.
A task of this nature cannot be settled off-hand, and was
peculiarly difficult at the time of the Return, for there was
no central authority with unquestioned influence which
could determine the question. I suggest that the verses under
review show one of the tentative efforts to bring about order,
before the final law in Numbers permanently decided the
usage which was to prevail. In my judgement, two features
in our account point to an earlier date for its composition.
Thus the author made no distinction between the provision
which was made for the priests and the levites respectively.
Full details were given of the sources from which the
revenues were drawn, but after these were collected it was
merely stated that they were devoted to the priests and
levites. This is in strong contrast with the terms of the law
in Numbers, where each source of revenue was ear-marked
and assigned to one or other of the separate orders. Again,
the author here was very conscious of the fact that the community comprised both Israelites and Judeans. Both were
represented, and both were doing their part to meet the
situation. But he was also conscious of a divergence of the
way in which they met the claims on them, for he set down
the sources from which Judah and Israel drew their offerings.

There is no uniform usage, as there is no homogeneous community. In these two respects the passage contrasts with the law in Numbers, which ordered a common practice for all Israel.

Now the features in which this passage differs from the law in Numbers are in agreement with the attitude of the Chronicler. C alone set priest and levite on an equal footing in regard to their status, and he alone was likely to make no sharp distinction between them in their claims on the temple-offerings. To him also we owe the account of Hezekiah's effort to bring the remanent Israelites into a common worship with their brethren in the South.

It has already been stated that the confused condition of chap. 31 must make any effort to bring it into order tentative at the best. In these circumstances it is advisable to ignore these conclusions in any attempt to sum up a general statement about Hezekiah's reform. The remaining chapters, however, show the sequence which has now become familiar. The narrative, which forms its basis, was the work of the Chronicler. Whatever may be its historical value, it represents his attitude and reflects his point of view. To this have been added a series of notes, which disturb the account, in one case producing a duplication, in other cases confusing the text. These cannot be combined into another narrative, which has been blended with the original. They convey no sense apart from the text in which they appear. The common element which appears in them all is that they were intended to bring C's account into agreement with the later law.

R

VI

THE CHRONICLER AND DEUTERONOMY

IT has long been recognized that the books of Chronicles show their author to have been acquainted with and strongly influenced by the book of Deuteronomy. Von Rad has collated one side of the evidence with such care that it is sufficient to refer a student to his book.[1] He has pointed out that terms which are common in, and even peculiar to, the earlier work reappear in the later, and that, especially in hortatory passages, the writer reproduced the familiar cadences and formulae of his predecessor. Yet it must be added that, so long as the evidence is confined to similarities of expression and taken from hortatory material, it does not reach very far, for it does not involve agreement with or dependence on the legislation which is peculiar to the Deuteronomic Code. Deuteronomy contains much more than a corpus of legislation: its law is framed in a series of expository, homiletic, and historical passages which intro-duce and conclude the statutes. This material, which con-tains, among much else that is valuable, one of the great utterances of Jewish religion, the Shᵉmaʿ, was excellently adapted to serve the purpose of a book of devotion. Indeed, this feature of the book may explain why it was preserved in its entirety in the Jewish Canon, long after its peculiar law had passed into desuetude and had given place to the final post-exilic law. Men could continue to use those devout and moving chapters, as both Jews and Christians can and do use them to this day. If a further proof were needed of the esteem in which those parts of the book were held, it might be found in the fact that they were not left in their original condition, but received additions from time to time, which show later writers using their contents for

---

[1] *Das Geschichtsbild des chronistischen Werkes.*

the guidance of their own generation.[1] Men do not annotate
and add to a volume which has already passed into oblivion;
they only pay such tribute to material which has proved itself
too useful to be forgotten.   Because the Chronicler did not
so much teach history as teach religion through history, he
was the more likely to be influenced by Deuteronomy, for
the book supplied to him what it can still supply to reverent
students.

The relation of the Chronicler to Deuteronomy will,
however, be very different in character, if it can be proved
that the resemblances between the two books are not confined to the hortatory passages, but extend to matters of
history and legislation.   What follows will deal only with
that subject, and before entering on certain larger considerations it may be well to group together a few minor
points which fall under the same heading.

When Jehoshaphat had to meet an invasion from Ammon,
Edom, and Moab he went up to the temple in the presence
of the congregation and offered prayer, II. 20: 1 ff.   In his
prayer he referred to the fact that Yahweh had not permitted
Israel at the conquest of Palestine to attack these three tribes,
v. 10.   This view of the situation appears in an itinerary
which was incorporated in Numbers and which derived
from E: it is also found in the historical introduction to the
book of Deuteronomy, c. 2.[2]   C was therefore familiar with
the tradition which formed the basis of that narrative.
Again, when C related David's victory over the Philistines
at the beginning of his reign, he told how the king captured
the gods of the enemy, I. 14: 8–17.   But while the author of
Samuel was content to say that the victor carried off these
gods, C was careful to add that David gave commandment, and they were burned with fire, v. 12.   When he did
this, he made the king follow the Deuteronomic law in
7: 5, 25.

[1] For the proof of the composite character of these chapters, cf. my
Deuteronomy: the Frame-work to the Code, passim.

[2] Cf. my *Deuteronomy: the Framework to the Code*, pp. 168 ff.

A larger question appears in the attitude taken by the two sources on the levites and their position. It has already been noted that C introduced levites as early as the period of David. From that time they are prominent in his narrative, according to which their activity was not confined to their religious duties, but extended to other spheres of the national life. Here, again, proof has been offered that the men were not subordinate to the priests in the exercise of any of these functions. The historian, further, wrote of them as having fulfilled their directly religious duties in both kingdoms until the schism under Jeroboam, and as having been possessed of rights in the kingdom of Israel.

It is important to contrast the prominence here given to this clerical order with the position assigned to them in the historical books. The first mention of levites occurs in the appendix to the book of Judges, where we hear of a levite having come north from Judah, and having been installed by Micah as his family priest. So highly were his services valued that members of the tribe of Dan, on their way to a new settlement, tempted him away to become priest at their clan-sanctuary, Judges c. 17 f.[1] After that the levites disappear from the early historical literature: the books of Samuel and Kings ignore them,[2] and leave the impression that the only servants of the cult were the priests, except that they mention door-keepers at the temple. As soon, however, as we turn to the book of Ezra, the situation is suddenly and unaccountably changed. The levites not only reappear, but they do so in a new character: they are no longer the sporadic wanderers of the book of Judges, but a clearly defined order who held an equally clearly defined position in the temple-worship. Their status was sharply distinguished from and made strictly subordinate to that of the priests. There is a hiatus here in the history of the priesthood, which obviously demands an explanation. The gap is

[1] I omit mention of the mysterious levite cc. 19 f., because nothing is told us about the man's origin, status, or functions.

[2] They appear once, 1 Sam. 6: 15.

wider when it is recognized that, according to the received opinion, the books of Chronicles were not yet in existence.

When now we turn from the historical books to those which contain the law, there is no difficulty in recognizing the legislation which agrees with the book of Ezra on this subject. The laws about the priesthood which appear in Exodus and Numbers ascribe to Moses the institution of the two orders in the cult of the tabernacle, and derive from his authority the subordination of the levites to the priests. So strong is their attitude on the question of the hierarchy that there are incorporated among them the accounts of two miracles, one of which vindicated the supremacy of the sons of Aaron, while the other related the doom which destroyed certain levites who dared to claim equality with the priesthood. On the other hand the Deuteronomic Code never called the priests the sons of Aaron and never referred to a hierarchy among the cult-officials. The absence from the Code of these two features which are prominent in the book of Ezra and the late law is the more noteworthy because they both appear in the late chapters of Deuteronomy, where it can be proved on other grounds that they have been introduced by a later hand. Instead of making the levite subordinate to the priest the Code used the two terms indifferently. Indeed, its characteristic phrase for describing the cult-officials was that of levitical priests, the meaning of which can only be that there were priests in the country who could not claim levitical descent. The law-givers refused to allow priests who could not claim descent from Levi, not priests who could not claim descent from Aaron, to serve at the sanctuary altars. For it forbade the faithful to resort to any sanctuary which was not served by these men, and it permitted any levite who came with all desire of his soul to become a ministrant at the altar.

This brief synopsis of the situation is sufficient to bring into relief the similarity between C and the Deuteronomic Code, which is the more noteworthy because, in the features which reveal their similarity, they both differ from the book of Ezra and the legislation in Exodus and Numbers. Neither of them called the priesthood the sons of Aaron, and neither spoke of a hierarchical order among the clergy. Both of them gave a high place, not only in the cult but in the more secular service of the community, to the levites. They differ, however, in two interesting particulars. The law-givers used the terms, priest and levite, indifferently, as though they were not conscious of any distinction: C, on the other hand, recognized both priests and levites as servitors in the temple. Again, the law-givers were conscious of the existence of priests who could not claim levitical descent, and found it necessary to warn the faithful against any recognition of them: there is no trace in C of such a distinction or of a similar danger.

The Chronicler made a sporadic use of the term, levitical priests.[1] The description is confined to him, to the Deuteronomic Code, and to Ezek. 44: 15. Its use in Ezekiel is peculiar, for he has defined the men as the sons of Zadok, and has continued by a statement of their functions, which the later law committed to the wider order of the sons of Aaron. He also gave a reason for the trust the men received: they kept the charge of My sanctuary, when *b*ᵉ*ne Yisrael* went astray from Me. In an earlier verse, v. 10, he declared the levites to have been involved in and largely responsible for this apostasy of Israel. Thus he drew a definite contrast between the levitical priests and the general levites, and agreed with the Deuteronomic Code in using the former expression for the legitimate order. He entirely departed from the Code—and from every one else—by making these

[1] How often he used it is uncertain. Evidently the later copyists were not very exact here, and were inclined to insert a *waw*, and so turned the expression into the more familiar: priests and levites. Instances appear where the M.T. reads levitical priests, while the LXX renders priests and levites: in other cases the exact opposite occurs; once or twice M.T. and LXX have levitical priests. The evidence is sufficient to prove that C employed the phrase, but is too uncertain to show that he attached a special sense to it.

legitimate priests a sept of the Aaronic order. C, on the other hand, followed the Code in the use of the term, and, so far as our evidence goes, applied it to the whole body of the levites.

Thus the attitude of the Chronicler on the subject of the composition of the levitical order and of their status relatively to the priests is not precisely the same as that of the Deuteronomic Code or of the book of Ezra. He occupies a middle position between the two. He distinguished between the two orders, and could speak of priests and levites when he wrote about the temple-cult, a distinction which is still unrecognized in the Code. He used the term, levitical priests, with a slightly different nuance from that which the words bear in the same document. But these distinctions, while they are interesting, are of less importance than those which mark off the law-givers and the historian from the author of Ezra. To confine the priesthood to one clan of the tribe of Levi and to constitute them into a privileged class stand in a different category. How revolutionary these changes were and how novel they once appeared can be gathered from the records of the two miracles by which, according to the late law-givers, they were enforced. To set this arrangement of the temple-officials under the authority of Moses and to safeguard it by relating the divine intervention to maintain it was to declare it the immutable law for Israel. Because it became the final use in the temple, the two documents which ignored it must have been written before it was adopted: and the writers of these two documents were nearer to one another in outlook and attitude than they were to those who followed them.

The question of the status of the levites is closely allied to that of the functions which were assigned to them. Instead of entering into a general discussion which might travel over trodden ground, it is only necessary to concentrate on two passages, both of which occur in the account of Hezekiah's reform. Reference has already been made to both in the earlier discussion, and attention has been directed to their departure from the terms of the later law.[1] Here it is necessary to point out their agreement with the book of Deuteronomy. In his exhortation to the levites, after he had committed to them the task of purifying the temple, Hezekiah concluded by saying: my sons, be not now negligent, for the Lord hath chosen you to stand before Him, to minister unto Him and that ye should be His ministers and burn incense, II. 29: 11. Except for the mention of burning incense, the functions of the levites are described in similar terms in the Code. In a regulation which dealt with the dues of the levitical priests the law-givers concluded with the statement: for the Lord thy God hath chosen him (i.e. Levi) out of all thy tribes to stand to minister in the name of the Lord, him and his sons for ever, 18: 5. Again, after the celebration of passover and the festival of unleavened bread the levitical priests, or the priests and the levites, arose and blessed the people, II. 30: 27. This finds a parallel in one of the early hortatory passages in Deuteronomy: at that time the Lord separated the tribe of Levi to bear the ark of the covenant of the Lord, to stand before the Lord to minister unto Him, and to bless in His name unto this day, 10: 8. The divergence between the functions committed to the levites here and in the later law is even more marked in the case of Deuteronomy than in that of the Chronicler. For the hortatory passage is put into the mouth of Moses, and the Code is said to have been delivered to Israel by Moses before the entry into Palestine. But here again Deuteronomy and C combine to occupy a position about the functions of the levites which does not agree with that of the later law, as they did in relation to the status of the same order. Here also such an attitude on the question points to the two documents having been written before that law was issued.

A peculiar feature of Deuteronomy is the interest its law-givers showed in bringing the distinctive law of Israel to the

---

[1] Cf. pp. 103 ff and 112.

knowledge of the members of the nation. Children were to receive instruction in the meaning of the rituals they witnessed. In order that the parents might be able to fulfil that duty the parents must themselves know the terms of the law they were to teach. Therefore the fundamental demands were to be inscribed on great stones at the first crossing of Jordan; others were cast into the form of a commination and read in the hearing of the people; at the end of every seven years, when the whole community had come together at the feast of booths, the law was to be read in their hearing. The men who were made responsible for reading the law were the levites, Deut. 27: 11–26, 31: 9–13. As Deuteronomy stands alone among the codes of law in providing for this necessity in the national life, so Chronicles differs from the other historical books in relating an effort which was made to meet the need. According to C, Jehoshaphat instituted a commission, the business of which was to teach the law in the towns of Judah, II. 17: 7–9, and this was largely composed of levites.

As these two sources displayed an interest in making known to the people the law which ought to govern their conduct, they were equally interested in the means of guaranteeing the enforcement of the law throughout the land. Deuteronomy commanded the institution of judges and officers 'in all thy gates', 16: 18–20: C credited Jehoshaphat with having instituted a court of first instance in all the provincial towns of Judah, II. 19: 5 ff. The instructions which the king gave to his new officers required them to consider their conduct, for they judged not for man, but for the Lord: the fear of the Lord must be before them and the recognition that there was no iniquity with Him, nor respect of persons nor taking of gifts. The language is closely parallel to that in the Code, where the judges shall not wrest judgement, nor respect persons, nor take a gift. C added that Jehoshaphat set up a court of final instance in the capital, and when he described the questions which might come before that tribunal in v. 10, he used terms which are again

paralleled in Deut. 17: 8 f., where there is mention of a
similar court. There is, however, a divergence in the description of the two courts which deserves attention, because it
throws light on the relation between C and the Code, and
even on the vexed question of the date and origin of Deuteronomy. When C described Jehoshaphat's action in the
matter he made his meaning unmistakable. The seat of
the court was at Jerusalem, its composition was defined, and
its sphere or competence was also marked off. It decided
all cases which arose in the capital and so far was on the
same level as the other courts in the provincial towns: but
it also acted as a court of final instance, since it had power to
decide on any cases which were appealed to it from the
local courts. The terms of Deut. 17: 8–13, on the other hand,
are much more vague. If any difficult case arose which
concerned matters of controversy 'within thy gates', men
were instructed to have recourse to 'the sanctuary which
the Lord thy God shall choose', where they could be sure
of finding 'the levitical priests and the judges who shall be
in those days'. They must accept the decision which was
there issued to them: and from the emphasis which is laid
on their acquiescing in the decision it is evident that one
aim in the legislation was to put an end to those bitter
quarrels which can poison the life of a village. When this
regulation is compared with the action ascribed to Jehoshaphat, two features appear which reveal a difference in the
situation described. The Code did not speak of a central
court and said nothing about Jerusalem. It bade men in a
local community, between whom a controversy had arisen
which they could not determine for themselves, carry the
question to a sanctuary where there was a competent judi-
catory; and ordered them to accept the decision. But since
the sanctuary which the Lord shall choose *may* not mean the
temple, and since there is no mention of the revision of
a previous decision, this does not imply the institution of a
court of final instance. The action which C ascribed to
Jehoshaphat developed and completed the legislation in the

Code, since it provided a court which was competent to unify the administration of justice in Israel. But while C referred the movement to a king of Judah and made it concern itself with Judah alone, he dissociated it from all connexion with Josiah's reform. It had nothing directly to do with the centralization of worship.[1]

Where the influence of Deuteronomy on C appears most clearly is in the double account of the celebration of passover at Jerusalem under Hezekiah and under Josiah. It is necessary to draw attention to certain features of these two passages.

In the discussion of Hezekiah's reform it has been pointed out that this is the earliest *historical* record of the change in locus for passover from the homes of the people to the sanctuary. It has also been noted that, by ascribing the change to Hezekiah, C did not conceive it to have been the outcome of the discovery of the book of the law in the time of Josiah. But one must go further and say that, instead of basing this alteration in one of the leading rites of the nation on that

[1] The orthodox view of this law in Deuteronomy sees in it evidence of the revision to which the Code was subjected in order to adapt it to the new conditions which followed the centralization of worship under Josiah. Two grave difficulties attend this explanation. The author of the passage in Chronicles who described the institution of a central court of justice at Jerusalem had no difficulty in making his meaning clear. On the other hand the men who revised the passage in Deuteronomy with the intention of describing the same court left its locus uncertain and said nothing about revising the decisions of the inferior courts. Yet it might have been expected that men who were revising an original document would be clear in the terms they used. Again, it is not easy to see why the centralization of sacrificial worship brought with it the institution of a court of the type which is described by the Chronicler. If the business which came before that court had been of a purely ecclesiastical character the connexion might have been understood. But both in Deuteronomy and Chronicles the cases dealt with were not confined to those of a religious character. Accordingly, as the court was required to deal with secular affairs, members of the laity were joined with representatives of the priesthood in deciding them, the judge in the one case, lay members in the other.

or on any other law book, the historian ascribed its adoption
in Judah to the decision of the king. Hezekiah issued the
letters of invitation to the remanent Israelites. When it
became evident that a postponement of the ceremony into
the second month was advisable it was again the king with
the support of the princes and the congregation, who decided
on the further change. When, again, some of the Israelites
incurred guilt through their want of the necessary ceremonial cleanness it was Hezekiah who interceded on their
behalf. Throughout the movement which changed the locus
of passover the king was the dominant figure. Further, when
he took this step, Hezekiah acted without precedent. In
other cases, when C described the conduct of the reforming
kings, he stated that the men restored the conditions which
had prevailed in the temple under David. In this case he
did not, for the simple reason that, according to his view of
the situation, he could not. After his description of the passover under Josiah he stated that there was no passover like
to it kept in Israel since the days of Samuel the prophet,
neither did any of the kings of Israel keep such a passover
as Josiah kept, II. 35: 18. The change of locus for passover
to the sanctuary was first effected in Judah by Hezekiah on
his own authority.

This gives significance to two suggestive hints as to the
way in which the proposed change was received in the
kingdom. One reason which is given for the postponement
of the ceremony into the second month is that the priests
had not sanctified themselves in sufficient numbers, II. 30: 3.
Their co-operation became necessary, as soon as what had
hitherto been a family rite was celebrated at the sanctuary.
The statement is made in order to explain why the ceremony
was postponed from its age-long date, and is combined with
another reason. It need not therefore involve any censure
on the priests, but may merely imply a hesitation on their
part to adopt the proposed change of locus, especially since
it emanated from no other authority than that of the king.
It was natural that men who were responsible for the

conduct of the cult, were not ready to accept so profound a change, and even hesitated in view of the new duties and responsibilities which it put upon their shoulders. In contrast with the unreadiness of the priests, C set down with a certain satisfaction that no opposition to the change appeared on the part of the laity, for the thing was right in the eyes of the king and of all the congregation, v. 4. Whatever their religious leaders may have thought or done, the worshippers in Judah offered no opposition to the royal enactments. The two statements on the attitude of priests and people, which are introduced together, show that the community were conscious of the novel character of the royal decree.

In the discussion of Hezekiah's reform it has also been pointed out that the leading feature of C's account of the passover is the desire Hezekiah showed that the remanent Israelites should share in the ceremony. The question at once arises how the king of Judah could ever have expected these men to come to any sanctuary for this particular rite. Had he invited the men to join their brethren in the festival of unleavened bread his action would have been explicable and even natural. For *mazzoth* was one of the three festivals at which every faithful Israelite was expected to resort to a sanctuary. The Judean king would then have offered the remanent Israelites the opportunity of taking part in one of those ancestral rites, which had been denied to them from the time when the Assyrian conquerors ravaged their country and destroyed its shrines. But if the men had been in the habit of celebrating passover in their own homes, this was the one outstanding ritual of their faith which, since it required neither priest nor altar, was unaffected by the conquest. Yet C's account emphasizes throughout that the royal invitation was to come to Jerusalem for passover; and when he mentioned the festival of *mazzoth* which followed he merely stated that the Israelites who remained in Jerusalem took part in that also. On the supposition that passover was a family rite in Israel, Hezekiah was not merely inviting the men to join their brethren in Judah: he was asking them to abandon their age-long practice in worship. He might hope to effect such a change in Judah, where he was the representative of the Davidic line; but he had no such influence among the men whom he was addressing. In spite of this, according to C, he not only issued the invitation but found some who were willing to accept it.

These considerations, in turn, give significance to a statement about the attitude of the remanent Israelites to passover, which appears in 30: 5. There it is said that the men had not kept it לרוב, in great numbers, or for a long time, in such sort as it is written. The remark follows directly on Hezekiah's invitation to come to Jerusalem, and is couched in such terms as to make it clear that the men's condition had interfered with the performance of their religious duties, especially in connexion with passover. But if the meaning was that since the time of the conquest the men had ceased to practise the rite altogether, it was unnecessary to add that they had not been practising it in such sort as it is written. That final clause must be interpreted in the light of the connexion in which it stands. On the one hand it must refer to some method of celebrating passover which had ceased because of the subject condition to which the Israelites had been reduced: on the other hand it must refer to the opportunity which Hezekiah was bringing within their reach by inviting them to join with their brethren at the temple. Not only so but, as far as the Israelites were concerned, the method of celebration which had ceased among them was said to be 'as it is written' in a regulation which they recognized.

Now there is only one law in the Pentateuch which connects passover with the sanctuary, and this definitely made the change of locus a novelty: thou mayest not sacrifice the passover within any of thy gates which the Lord thy God giveth thee: but at the place which the Lord thy God shall choose to make His name to dwell in, there thou shalt sacrifice the passover, Deut. 16: 5 f. If the Deuteronomic

Code be recognized as the law of northern Israel, all the difficulties in connexion with C's account of Hezekiah's action disappear. The Israelites had been in the habit of celebrating passover at a sanctuary, as it was written. The Assyrian conquest had made it impossible to practise the rite because their sanctuaries were wrecked. They had not therefore been able to celebrate after the 'sort' which their law commanded, but which the Judean king brought within their reach. Hezekiah in his action was not inviting the men to surrender their ancestral practice and to join their brethren in the south in a method of celebration which was as novel to them as it was to Judah. Nor is it necessary to ask what authority a Judean king could have had which might lead him to suppose that Israel would make so great a change at the mere invitation of an outsider. He could invite the men to fulfil the regulations of their own law when he offered them the opportunity to come to Jerusalem.

The Chronicler separated the change of locus in passover from all connexion with the book of the law which was found in the temple, since he made Hezekiah introduce the change in Judah: he also acknowledged the authority of the Deuteronomic Code in northern Israel.[1]

The outstanding peculiarity of C's account of Josiah's passover, as has already been noted, is the detailed descrip-

---

[1] I may be pardoned for adding a note, though it is not strictly germane to the subject under discussion. Rudolph in his recent discussion of the *Elohist von Exodus bis Josua* has examined the double law about passover which appears in Exodus, c. 12, and has expressed agreement with the common opinion according to which the earlier of these, vv. 1–14, is referred to P. Yet, if that law is made post-exilic or even post-Josianic, the remarkable feature of it is that it makes no reference to sanctuary, altar, or priest. Passover retains its primitive character and bears no trace of the change which must have come over it, as soon as it was transferred to the temple. Nor is this all, for unlike the rest of P's legislation it is not referred to Moses, but is retained as a rite which was practised in Egypt. Thus it antedated sanctuary, altar, and priest, as it demanded none of the three. A law of this character must be earlier than the post-exilic period.

tion which he gave of the use which was followed in the celebration. Since, however, the event formed part of the king's larger work of reform, it may be well, before entering on an analysis of the chapter which described that use, to recognize the divergence of the two sources in the order in which they placed the successive stages of the reform. According to C, Josiah began to seek the Lord in the eighth year of his reign, when he was 16 years old, II. 34: 3. In the twelfth year he began the purification of the land, and carried it out from Judah and Jerusalem to Ephraim, Manasse, and Simeon, as far as Naphtali, vv. 3–7. This must mean the twelfth year of the reign, since it is stated in v. 8 that the work of the temple repairs, which began in the eighteenth year of the reign, followed the purification of the land and the house. The verses which describe that purification *may* be a much abbreviated version of II Kings 23: 4–20, since both accounts end with the clause 'and he returned to Jerusalem'. In the eighteenth year of the reign, at the age of 26, the king proceeded to the repair of the temple, which led to the discovery of the book of the law and the consultation of the prophetess, vv. 8–28. After this appears the account of the royal covenant in the temple, vv. 29–32. The king's work for reform of religion is then summed up in v. 33: Josiah took away all the abominations out of all the countries that pertained to the children of Israel and made all that were found in Israel to serve, even to serve the Lord their God. All his days they departed not from following the Lord, the God of their fathers. After this follows the description of the royal passover which is introduced with the abrupt statement: and Josiah kept a passover unto the Lord at Jerusalem. No date is given except in the concluding sentence, 35: 19.

On the other hand K began with the king's eighteenth year, but whether of his reign or of his age is not stated. In that year Josiah initiated the temple repairs, II. 22: 3, which brought to light the book of the law on the purport of which the prophetess was consulted. This was followed by the covenant in the temple, 23: 1–3, and that in turn by the purification of the temple in which the covenant had just been instituted and by the purification of the land of Palestine, vv. 4–20. Thereafter Josiah instituted the pass-over, as it was written in this book of the covenant, and he put away them that had familiar spirits and the wizards and the teraphim and the idols and all the abominations that were spied in the land of Judah and in Jerusalem that he might perform the words of the law which were written in the book that Hilkiah the priest found in the house of the Lord, vv. 21–4.

The order of events in K obviously raises grave difficulties. As it stands it has compressed the entire work of Josiah's reform into one year of hectic activity, 22: 3, 23: 23, whereas C was able to allow six years for the purification of the temple and of the land of Palestine, before the temple repairs were taken in hand. It has made the king begin to repair the temple before the sanctuary was purified, which involves the admission that the covenant into which the pious king brought his people was concluded in the presence of heathen emblems. These questions must, however, be left to students of the text of the book of Kings. What is more strictly rele-vant to the present inquiry is to note the effect of the order of events, as that appears in K. It brought the royal series of reforms into integral relation to the law by making them the consequence of the discovery. Only after the momen-tous discovery did Josiah set on foot the purification of the temple and the land. He also instituted the passover at Jerusalem in agreement with this book of the covenant; and he proceeded to another purge of Judah and Jerusalem, about which it is said that it was on the basis of this law. Naturally, since the successive reforms were carried out in obedience to the book, the starting-point for all Josiah's activity must have been its discovery in the temple. On the other hand, the discovery of the book with the resultant covenant stands isolated in the account of the Chronicler, and is brought into no integral relation to the work of reform. The purification of the temple and of the land had been effected before its discovery, and the clause which connected passover with the law-book is absent. The Chronicler credited Hezekiah with having begun the movement for associating Judah and Israel in worship at the temple and for changing the locus of passover, and so separated these two reforms from any connexion with the book of the law. When he described Josiah's later reforms he did not describe the royal action as founded on this discovery. It is even a suspicious circumstance that, while the records differ widely in their general attitude, the block of material which describes the discovery of the book is practically identical in its terms in the two sources.

In his brief account of Josiah's passover K made no reference to the presence of men from Israel, and stated that the rite was celebrated at Jerusalem. C, on the other hand, did not mention the locus, but twice stated that men from Israel were among the worshippers, 35: 17 f. He also noted that passover was combined with the festival of unleavened bread, v. 17, and added that the event took place on the fourteenth day of the first month, v. 1. Since there was no obvious reason for mentioning the exact day of the festival it may be supposed that he was contrasting the celebration under Josiah with that which was instituted by Hezekiah. Nor did he require to explain the presence of members of Israel, since their right to be present had already been established. There was, therefore, no need to summon these men: the custom had been assured. The one requirement laid down by the earlier king, that Israel should repent and return to the Lord, had been satisfied. Their land had been purged of its heathen emblems, and under the influence of the new reform its inhabitants had turned to serve the Lord their God, nor did they during Josiah's reign turn back from following the God of their fathers, 34: 33.

The initiative on the occasion, as in the case of Hezekiah's passover, was taken by the king. He kept the passover, and did not need, like his predecessor, to consult either his princes or the congregation at Jerusalem. Under the earlier king a celebration at the temple was a novelty, the invitation to the Israelites was unexampled, and the change of date was an interference with the practice of the nation. Under the later king the change of locus had already been effected, the inclusion of the members of the northern kingdom had been accepted, and there was no need to alter the date, since that alteration had arisen from the special conditions in Hezekiah's time. On C's view of the course of events, Josiah needed to do no more than follow the example of his predecessor. Also, as the earlier king had issued instructions to the temple-clergy about their functions, the later king issued similar instructions to the same men: in both cases the instructions were chiefly given to the levites. Josiah bade them follow the practice under David and Solomon by dividing themselves into courses. They would thus be able to serve the successive relays of worshippers who are here called their brethren, 35: 4 f.[1]

The description of the use at Josiah's passover has received a great deal of attention from scholars. Though they differ widely in the results at which they arrive, they all agree that the account is so confused in its character and shows such signs of inconsistency in its attitude that it cannot be accepted in its present form. No modern commentator fails to recognize that the chapter has received a good deal of revision.

The account began with the statement that the levites were instructed to slay the paschal victims and prepare for their brethren according to the divine command issued by Moses, v. 6. An apparent parallel to this appears in the record of Hezekiah's passover at 30: 17, but there it was stated that the levites slew the victims for those of the laity

[1] It may be necessary here to add that I hold no brief for the historical accuracy of the account of Hezekiah's reform. My one concern is to point out the self-consistency of C's narrative, when it is examined by itself and as a whole.

who were ceremonially unclean, which implies that, except in such cases, the older custom of each head of a father's house slaying the lamb for his household was maintained. No law which committed the slaying of the victims to the levites appears in the Mosaic torah. It is possible that, when the locus of passover was changed to the sanctuary, the practice as to slaughter may have varied, and that at one time the task was committed to the clergy and this ritual form was put under the authority of Moses. The question will then arise as to the precise meaning of the brethren for whom the levites were thus to prepare. If the phrase means the worshippers, as in the preceding verse, the direction may imply that the levites completed the preparation of the victims, and so presided over the ceremony. If, however, these brethren were the priests, the slaying of the victims was the mere preliminary to the manipulation of the blood, which in vv. 10 f. was reserved to those priests. On the earlier explanation the instruction may belong to the original: on the second it may be an addition preparing for the later verses, which gave the priests not a place, but the leading place in the ritual. While the question cannot be determined without an examination of the following instructions, certain indications point to the verse being an interpolation. Thus it is at least peculiar to find in two consecutive verses the brethren of the levites used for the general body of the worshippers and for the priesthood. Allied to this is the sudden emergence of the priests on the scene at the opening of a series of instructions directed to the levites. Again, the appearance of an appeal to the authority of the Mosaic law immediately after a reference to the practice of David and Solomon is reminiscent of other cases which have already been noted, where such an appeal to the Mosaic law was the sign of a reviser.

The paschal victims for the occasion were provided by the king, who gave his to the people, by the princes who destined theirs for the people, for the priests, and for the

levites, by the rulers of the temple on behalf of the priests,
and by the leading levites for their brother levites, vv. 7–9.
The last two verses have been suspected of being composite
and have been assigned to separate sources. Thus it has
been noted that v. 8a mentions the liberality of the secular
princes to the people, the priests, and the levites, but does
not, as in the other three cases, mention the amount of their
gifts. In his commentary Kittel judged it possible to make
the people parallel to the priests and levites, but he evidently
came to feel this artificial, for in *B.H.* Edit. II he proposed
to omit the clergy. Since, however, there was no obvious
reason for inserting the mention of the priests and levites, the
deletion appears arbitrary. In vv. 8 b 9 Kittel holds that,
when the author detailed the gifts of the priestly and levitical
leaders to the lower clergy, he wished to substitute priestly
leaders for the secular princes. He therefore made this an
addition. Yet C took no umbrage at the princes' offerings
on the occasion of Hezekiah's passover, 30: 24: nor does the
author of Ezra show any reluctance in detailing gifts to the
sanctuary from the same donors. Benzinger, on the other
hand, would omit the clerical offerings as a later addition:
in his view some one missed any mention of the clergy having
borne their part in the great event. But why drag in a later
hand? Surely it is not impossible that the original author
marked the significance of the national passover by making
all the leaders of the people, secular and clerical, generous
in their contributions to it. There is no sufficient ground for
suspecting the verses.

Of much greater significance is it to note that the paschal
victims were taken from the צאן or lambs and kids, and
בקר or larger cattle. The donors gave animals taken
from both these classes לפסחים i.e. as passover victims.
Now Deuteronomy 16: 2 is the only law which permitted
the passover to be taken from the flock or the herd.

There follows a description of the preparation of the
victims, vv. 11 f. The worshippers slew the animals, the
priests manipulated the blood, and the levites skinned

the carcasses. Since the first verb is indefinite and has no subject, and since the share of the two classes of the clergy in the
ritual is defined, this is a legitimate rendering of the verse.
Yet the disagreement between the procedure here and that
which was ordered in v. 6 is patent. It serves to confirm
the impression that v. 6 is a later addition. I suggest that
it is possible to trace three stages in the development of the
ritual which was observed at passover. So long as the rite
was practised in the homes of the nation, the house-father
acted as priest; he slew the victim and manipulated the
blood by dashing it against the lintel and door-posts of the
house, as in Exod. c. 12. With the change in locus came a
change in the method, especially in relation to the blood.
Since the house had disappeared and with it the lintel and
the door-posts, the blood was treated like that of any other
sacrifice, it was now dashed against the altar by the priests.
But the custom of lay slaughter was retained. That is C's
view of the situation in v. 11. At a later date, however, the
entire preparation of the victims came into the hands of the
clergy, the levites slaying them and the priests manipulating
the blood, as in v. 6. That this was considered the final stage
was marked by its being put under the authority of Moses.

The following verses, however, present a much more
difficult and involved problem. There are two questions
which, for the sake of clarity, may be separately discussed.
The first concerns the source and purpose of certain burnt-
offerings which appear in vv. 12, 14, 16, and the relation
these must be supposed to have held to the passover. Alongside these burnt-offerings appear what are called the holy
offerings, v. 13, which were of an entirely different character,
since instead of being consumed on the altar they were
boiled and distributed among the worshippers, more after
the fashion of the *shelamim*. What connexion did these have
with the passover on the one side and with the burnt-
offerings on the other? At the first mention of the burnt-
offerings it is stated that they were removed and were
handed over to the worshippers in order to be offered to the

Lord, and so in regard to the cattle. The arrangement is said to have been according to the book of Moses, v. 12. The only source in the text from which these offerings can have been derived is the animals dedicated by the king and the leaders of the nation: but these were expressly destined as paschal victims. The diversion of a number of these animals from their original purpose to serve as burnt-offerings cannot have been according to the book of Moses. For the sacrificial calendar in Num. c. 29 makes no mention of burnt-offerings at the celebration of passover, as in v. 16 here: in this respect passover forms an exception among all the other festivals, major or minor.[1] What makes the reference to the book of Moses more peculiar is to find it stated in v. 16 that all the service of the Lord was prepared, to keep the passover and to offer burnt-offerings, according to the commandment of king Josiah. Even if it were supposed that the animals destined for burnt-offerings were selected from the paschal victims of the king and the leaders it is necessary to ask when the separation was made. As the text stands this was done after the paschal victims had been killed, had been drained of blood, and had been skinned. In that case the ritual prescribed by the book of Moses was not followed, for the feature of the burnt-offering in the law was that it was a holocaust. Finally the two words with which the verse closes, וכן לבקר and so they did to the cattle, are quite mysterious.[2]

In view of these difficulties the verse must be suspected to be the addition of a reviser, and this demands closer attention to the later mention of the burnt-offerings. In v. 14 the writer wished to explain why the levites were credited

---

[1] For a similar appearance of these offerings at Hezekiah's passover, cf. p. 111.

[2] When LXX[Ch] translated εις το πρωι and LXX[Esd] πρωινον they evidently read לַבֹּקֶר for לָבָּקָר; but the two words are sufficiently cryptic in their position without being made even more mysterious in their sense. I *suggest* that we should carry back the words and read them at the close of v. 11.

with having prepared the passover victims for themselves and for the priests. The reason he gave was that the priests were busy with the burnt-offerings. But that this explanation of the situation was secondary is clear from the repetition of the statement about the work of the levites, as well as from the fact that the priests were given the special title of sons of Aaron. When, again, the clause about the burnt-offerings is removed from v. 16, there remains the statement that all the service of the Lord was prepared, to keep the passover, according to the commandment of king Josiah. This is in agreement with the main narrative which made the king keep the passover, v. 1, and which stated that the service was prepared according to the royal commandment, v. 10. On the other hand the burnt-offerings were presented as it is written in the book of Moses, v. 12.

The perplexity of a student is, however, increased by the appearance of a third form of offering in v. 13. These, which are called holy offerings, cannot have been the animals dedicated for the purposes of passover, because the paschal victims are said to have been roasted with fire, while the others were boiled in cooking-vessels. As little can they have been the burnt-offerings, because not only was the flesh boiled, but it was afterwards distributed among the worshippers. Both methods of treating the flesh constituted a breach of the law as to burnt-offerings. Nor do the peace-offerings supply a parallel to the ritual described here. These holy offerings stand entirely without parallel, not merely in the ritual of passover, but in all the ordinary sacrificial system.

The mention of these holy offerings brings forward the second major difficulty in connexion with the passover, viz. the method in which the flesh of the victims was treated. The distinction in the verse appears at first to be very clear. The worshippers or the clergy—the verb is indeterminate— בשלו באש or 'roasted with fire' the passover: the holy offerings בשלו 'they sod' in pots, caldrons, and pans. In the former case it is noted that the treatment of the flesh of the paschal victims was כמשפט or according to the ordinance. The same

could not be said about the holy offerings, because there is
no ordinance prescribing sacrifices of this peculiar character.
On the other hand there are two ordinances which define
the method of preparing the flesh of the paschal victims.
In Exod. 12: 9 it was commanded: Eat not of it raw, nor
sodden at all with water, בשל מבשל במים, but צלי באש, roast
with fire. In Deut. 16: 7 the legislators were content to order
thou shalt בשל the flesh and eat it.

Now the ordinance to which the writer appeals seems to
be the regulation in Exod. 12: 9, with which it is in general
agreement. But there are two peculiar features in his
apparent quotation from this law. He did not use the
word צלי 'roasted with fire', which made the meaning of
the earlier command unmistakable, and he did use בשל,
the word used for the method definitely forbidden by the
legislators. He qualified the ambiguous word by adding
'in the fire' but, when he thus defined it, he used an expression which is without parallel elsewhere. He went on to
describe other offerings which were treated in the forbidden
method, and made his meaning very clear by the statement
that these were boiled in cooking-vessels. But the holy
offerings which he mentioned are without example elsewhere, and especially are absent from the ordinance to
which he appealed. One cannot fail to ask why, when he
referred back to Exod. 12: 9, he did not quote its exact and
unmistakable terms, but introduced an expression employed
in the passage to describe a usage which it forbade. One
must continue by asking why he introduced a set of offerings
treated in the forbidden manner, which were not mentioned in the ordinance to which he made his appeal.

Elsewhere בשל appears either with no qualifying word,
or with the addition of the vessel which was employed for
the purpose. There is no other instance where it occurs
with the addition of 'in the fire'. So invariable is the usage
that Driver in his note on the passage in Deuteronomy[1]
acknowledged that the usual and natural sense of the word

[1] In the *I.C.C.*

was 'boil'. He also noted that Exod. 12: 9 used the verb for the boiling which it forbade, and chose a different word for the roasting which it prescribed. He satisfied himself, however, by a reference to our verse, and quieted his exegetical conscience by saying that, since Chronicles was late, its account must represent the final and uniform method of dealing with the flesh. He did not, however, examine the context in which the verse appeared and so, not recognizing the difficulties which crowd round its interpretation, did not allow for the possibility that the account was not homogeneous. But the evidence for revision in the chapter is too plain to be ignored: and a record of such a character cannot be accepted in order to give a Hebrew word a sense which contradicts, *teste* Driver, its usage throughout the Old Testament. This is especially the case in view of the equally unexampled appearance of those holy offerings in the passover ritual. The only explanation which does justice to the facts of the case is to recognize here again the hand of the reviser. He found in the text the Deuteronomic description of the treatment of the flesh of the paschal victims, and brought it into agreement with Exod. 12: 9 by adding 'in the fire, according to the ordinance'. He explained the use of the forbidden word בשל by introducing the holy offerings, other than the paschal victims, which were sodden in pots, caldrons, and pans.[1]

At two points, then, the account gave offence to a later reviser. He objected to the presence of cattle among the paschal victims, and therefore he turned them into burnt-offerings, though the law did not provide for sacrifices of that character at passover. He objected to the statement that

---

[1] For a different interpretation of the offerings, burnt and holy, see Nikolsky's erudite and exhaustive article in *Z.A.W.* 1927, p. 245. The weakness of the article is that Nikolsky has not faced the difficulties in the passage which have been detailed, nor has he sufficiently allowed for the extent to which the chapter has been revised. It is interesting and instructive to compare the Rabbinical attempts to reconcile and explain these difficulties in *Pesach* 6: 3, 4.

these victims were prepared in any other way than by roasting: so he described passover as carried out after the Exodus ordinance and separated the paschal lambs from what were called holy offerings which were boiled and distributed to the worshippers. But the use of animals from the herd and permission to boil the flesh were precisely the elements in the Deuteronomic Code about passover in which it differed from the regulations in Exodus.

At some period, whether under Hezekiah or under Josiah, the practice of celebrating passover at the temple was adopted by the priesthood at Jerusalem. It had already been made the law in the northern kingdom, where the Deuteronomic Code was in force. Since the leading feature of that Code was to enforce *kultische Reinheit*, not *kultische Einheit*, and since the change of locus for passover had no essential relation to the centralization of sacrificial worship, the motive behind the law was probably to avoid abuses which were creeping into the household ritual, because it was uncontrolled by any authority. The change to the sanctuary ensured a purer and more uniform observance of the rite. What motive may have led to the adoption of the change in Judah it is impossible to determine, and in the present study it would be beyond our province to speculate. But two things are clear about the Chronicler's view of the way in which the change of locus was effected. According to him, the movement had nothing to do with the centralization of worship at Jerusalem, for he dated it in the reign of Hezekiah, and he separated Josiah's passover from any connexion with the book of the law found in the temple. He also made the initiative in both cases come from the king. Hezekiah instituted the change on his own authority, and even found his priesthood somewhat reluctant to support it. Josiah kept the passover, and all the service of the Lord in connexion with it was according to the commandment of the king. The use followed in the administration of the rite, according to C, conformed to the Deuteronomic Code in two particular usages which were peculiar to that law.

When the exiles returned to Jerusalem, they were not prepared to allow that so large a change in the form of worship
had had its origin in the royal authority, however pious the
individual king may have been. Therefore they revised
the Chronicler's account of Josiah's reforms, and made the
alteration in passover to have been the outcome of the law
which was discovered in the temple. The initiative in
matters of ritual was transferred from the king to the priests
who found that law and who recommended it to Josiah.
They, further, insisted that the ritual which was followed at
the administration must conform to the use which had
prevailed at passover in Judah. Therefore they revised the
Chronicler's account of Josiah's passover, and removed
from it the two obnoxious features in which it reproduced
the characteristic elements of the Deuteronomic Code.

VII

CONCLUSION

IT only remains to gather up the results as to the composition and date of the book which have emerged from the preceding analysis of the work of the Chronicler.

There is then clear evidence that the books of Chronicles, in the form in which we possess them, are not homogeneous but reveal the presence of more than one hand. Some of the material which has been added is of minor importance and may be classed with the glosses which are common in old documents. But it has become increasingly apparent that two writers have been mainly responsible for the book, and that the conclusion which Von Rad and the present writer had already reached, viz. that there are two main *Schichten* or strands representing a difference of attitude on important questions, has been justified, so far as the section of Chronicles to which attention has here been confined is concerned.[1] All the sections into which this study has been divided, except the second, bear the same testimony, though in differing degree. It becomes possible to set the two strands alongside each other and to estimate their character as literary documents. When this is done a marked difference is apparent between them. In the one case we find a self-consistent narrative, which records the history of the kingdom in Judah from the accession of David, and which can be read continuously. Except that it omitted all mention of the kingdom in Israel, the account runs parallel to that in the books of Samuel and Kings, and can be compared with its predecessor. Though the author regarded the king-

---

[1] In my judgement the same clearly marked distinction into two strands does not appear in the opening nine chapters, and its absence there forms an additional reason for separating this material from what follows. Unless I have misunderstood Von Rad, he makes his conclusion about the duality of authorship and outlook run through the whole book.

dom from a different point of view, and used great freedom in dealing with his original source in order to adapt it to this point of view, he preserved the outward form of a historical narrative. He also added a considerable amount of new material, but he wove this into his record of events with such success that he has given his book a unity and an outward cohesion. The situation is different when we combine the passages which have been assigned to the second strand in Chronicles. These do not form a continuous narrative of the kingdom, since they are entirely absent from several of the reigns. Nor can they be read continuously, for they are dependent for their sense on the narrative in which they have been embedded. At times this strand consists of no more than a clause or a few verses: at other times it broadens into a longer statement. But whether the passages are longer or shorter, they remain fragments and disconnected fragments because, after they have been separated from their context, they present no coherent meaning. The cohesion between them consists in their inward unity, in the common attitude they present on certain important issues: but apart from this, they remain fragmentary in their character. The natural conclusion from this situation is that Chronicles is not composed of two independent documents, dealing with the same subject, which have afterwards been combined. The relation between the two strands in the book is that of an original narrative, covering the period of the kingdom, which has at a later date been subjected to a careful and thorough revision.

This revision, however, it must next be noted, did not extend to the whole of the original document. There are certain sections in which no evidence of its presence is apparent, and for that reason no reference has been made to these in the preceding study. Thus the history of the kings who followed Josiah has been treated in a perfunctory fashion. The author hurried over the story of their reigns, contenting himself with abbreviating the material in Kings and presenting no more than a summary. Nor has he introduced any of his characteristic additions in the record, except in the case of Zedekiah, where he noted that the fall of the kingdom was due to the sin of the priests and the disobedience of the king to the message of Jeremiah. There is no sign of a later revision there. The same thing is true in connexion with the account of the life and activity of some of the minor kings. Again, the collection of prophetic messages, in which the original author conveyed his view of the relation of prophecy to the kingdom, as well as his conviction as to the cause of the kingdom's collapse, has been left practically untouched. There may be some few signs of the reviser's hand in the oracles themselves, but there are no such signs in the historical narratives which frame the messages, though these depart widely from the parallel accounts in Kings. Finally, the long account of David's life has been treated in a significant fashion. The account of his accession, his place as founder of the kingdom and of the Davidic dynasty, the record of his secular activities and of his success, his appointment of his successor are all left as in the original narrative. But so soon as the historian referred to the king's relation to the temple and the national worship, the annotator's work begins to appear. The first sign of his activity is present in the story of the transference of the ark to Jerusalem and, so long as the temple is only in preparation and has not yet come into existence, his notes are sporadic and consist of little more than changes in the text and short notes inserted in the story. When, however, we reach the instructions as to the future temple and its personnel which David delivered to his successor, and the later description of the way in which Solomon carried out these instructions, the evidence of the presence of a double strand becomes much more patent. In the same way, whenever the narrative dealt with the work of one of the reforming kings, the same phenomenon recurs: interpolations increase, annotations multiply, and we find duplications of incidents in connexion with the cult which betray a different point of view.

Again, the natural conclusion from this is that the annotator was no more a historian than the writer whom he annotated. He accepted the narrative of his predecessor, even where it diverged from the record in Kings, and neither added to it nor corrected anything in it. He agreed also with the verdict on the kingdom, and adopted the judgement that it had passed away because of the failure of the Davidic kings to obey the divine voice through the prophets. To him the enduring service which the dynasty had done for the nation lay in the fact that it had built and supported the temple. There he had nothing to add or to change. But the moment the record touched upon the temple, its origin, its history, its arrangements, its cult, and above all its personnel, his attention was awake. These, it will be noted, were precisely the subjects which his predecessor had introduced into his narrative and which find no parallel in the books of Kings. When, therefore, the annotator accompanied all this material with a series of notes and corrections and caveats, he was not attempting to plead for a more accurate reproduction of the practice of the past. We are in the presence of two men who held divergent views on the temple, its cult, and its personnel. The annotator profoundly disagreed with the attitude of the book he revised, and was diligent to correct its statements in order to bring them into line with his own convictions on the subject. The original narrative of the Chronicler was the earlier of the two strata in the book, and has been supplemented with the purpose of bringing it into agreement with a different view on the temple.

As soon as this relation between the two strata has been recognized it becomes necessary to define, so far as this is possible, the leading points of divergence between them. Here, if we ignore minor details, certain broad facts emerge from the preceding analysis. Thus the two writers held quite different views on the origin and the history of the temple. According to C, the first sanctuary in Jerusalem was the shrine which David prepared for the reception of

the ark, and which he set up entirely on his own initiative.
Because its tent of curtains was unworthy of Him who was
worshipped there, the king desired to replace it by a house
of cedar. Such a structure had been unknown in the past:
'in all places wherein I have walked with all Israel, spake I
ever a word with any of the judges of Israel, whom I commanded to feed My people, saying, why have ye not built
me a house of cedar?' Thus the temple had no predecessor,
except the tent over the ark. Though David himself was
not permitted to build, he received the promise that his son
was to carry out the design, and the תבנית or plan of the
new building was divinely revealed to him. Because the
temple involved so novel a change in Israel's worship, it
demanded and received the divine approval, and its structure must conform to the divine pattern. Therefore David
received both the approval of his purpose and the plans after
which it must be carried out. On the other hand to the
reviser the temple was no novelty; it merely reproduced the
tabernacle which had led the Israelites through the wilderness, and which had found a temporary resting-place at the
high place in Gibeon. Nor was there need for a new plan
of the future sanctuary, for the תבנית of the tabernacle had
been revealed by God to Moses. The temple was the permanent substitute for the tabernacle in which God sojourned
when He accompanied His people in their wanderings.
Now that He had given them rest in their own land He
took up His abode in the sanctuary chosen out of the tribes
of Israel where He caused His name to dwell.

Of the same character is the norm to which appeal is made
in the two strata of the book. As the Chronicler made David
receive the plan of the sanctuary from divine revelation, so
he stated that the king made all the arrangements for the
future conduct of the worship and that in these matters he
was also divinely guided. It was unnecessary to seek for
higher authority in regard to his enactments. Therefore,
when C described the conduct of the pious kings of the
Davidic line in relation to the temple, he was satisfied to say

that they restored the conditions which had prevailed there during the time of their great predecessor. On the other hand, the final authority to which the reviser appealed was the law which the Lord delivered unto Moses, either at Horeb or in the wilderness. The arrangements made in all matters connected with the temple were no more novel to Israel in the time of David than the temple itself. They had been instituted for the service of the tabernacle, and were simply continued in the sanctuary which had taken the place of the tabernacle. Whenever, also, it is possible to trace the annotator's successive judgements on these matters, they are found to be in agreement with the legislation in Exodus and Numbers, and they reflect the situation which, according to the author of the book of Ezra, prevailed in the temple after the Return. This is especially true in all questions relating to the relative status of the priests and the levites, a subject on which the attitude of the authors of the two strata in the book is most markedly divergent.

Again, a similar wide divergence appears in the attitude which the two writers took to the ark. That sacred emblem was to the Chronicler an object of reverence in itself. One of the first acts of David's reign was to transfer it to Jerusalem, and to make it the centre of the first cult which was instituted in the capital: his final words were the charge he gave Solomon to bring it and the vessels employed in its service to its final resting-place. When the new sanctuary was completed the ark was brought into it, and as soon as sacrifices had been offered before it, the glory of the Lord filled the temple as a token of the divine approval. The ark was thus an essential element in the temple-cult according to the Chronicler since, although David had on his own initiative brought it up to the shrine which he prepared for it, he had been divinely guided in the arrangements he made for its deposition in the temple. The reverence he thus gave the sacred emblem was allied, on the one side, with his view of the temple, since he made the new sanctuary a surrogate for the tent at the older shrine, and it was, on the other, linked with the status he assigned to the levites, for they alone possessed the privilege of acting as porters and servitors to the ark. The reviser had no similar estimate of the dignity of the emblem. According to him, the ark had no sooner reached the temple than it disappeared from the sight of the worshippers, and there its sole title of respect consisted in the fact that it contained the tablets of the law. The sacrifices which attended the dedication of the sanctuary were offered on the altar, and not till then did the glory of the Lord fill the house. In one place he made the ark no more than one of the vessels in the tabernacle. Here again he was in agreement with the law in Exodus, which made the tabernacle instead of the ark the guide of the nation through the desert, and which, though it never specified the purpose which it served, included the ark among the vessels of the tabernacle.[1]

The annotator therefore belonged to the generation which followed the Return from Exile, and was a convinced supporter of the polity which was adopted at the time when the temple was rebuilt. Whether we believe this law to have been a creation of the priests in Babylonia, which was brought to Jerusalem by Ezra and imposed by him on his co-religionists, or whether we believe it to have been essentially the usage of the Solomonic temple, adapted and developed to meet the new conditions, the generation in which it became the norm for Jewish life and worship is not doubtful. There may have been later modifications of its terms, but the broad lines of the new polity were determined within that generation. The legislation was codified and placed under the authority of Moses in the combination of history and law which occupies most of the books of Exodus and Numbers: and the book of Ezra is practically the official record of the course of events which accompanied its

[1] For further proof of the degradation of the ark from its earlier position, cf. my *Post-Exilic Judaism*, pp. 230 f., 240 f. Rudolph has recently shown himself conscious of the situation in the book of Exodus, cf. *Der Elohist von Exodus bis Josua*, pp. 55 ff.

acceptance in the community. Since the reviser accepted and appealed to the authority of this law, and since his annotations practically form a running commentary intended to superimpose its decisions on the longer narrative in Chronicles, the work of the Chronicler must have predated the final settlement, and offers another proof that the difficult questions which attended its decision were not settled with the promptitude and ease which appear in the book of Ezra. Instead of his book being the latest material in the Old Testament, it must be set alongside the proposals in Ezekiel as one of the programmes which were put forward, before the final settlement was reached.

When this earlier date is assigned to his work, the dependence of C on Deuteronomy, which has always been recognized, admits of an easier explanation, since the later the material is placed in its date, the more difficult does it become to understand why its author showed so much interest in a law book which had been superseded in authority. So long as the evidence for this Deuteronomic element in the book was confined to the reproduction of the peculiar phraseology of the older code, or was chiefly drawn from the hortatory passages, it was possible to account for its appearance from the peculiar character of Deuteronomy itself, which was admirably adapted to remain a book of devotion even when its authority as a code had ceased. But the use C made of Deuteronomy was not confined to passages of this character. I have no desire to overpress, or even to base upon, the conclusions in chap. vi as to the relation between the use followed at Josiah's celebration of passover and the ritual prescribed in the Deuteronomic Code, though they at least offer an explanation of a peculiarly confused and puzzling passage. Those results are novel and must be further tested before they can form a basis for other conclusions. But enough remains to make it clear that the relation between C and Deuteronomy goes beyond the use of the language of the book, and implies a knowledge and acknowledgement of its peculiar legislation. Nor is this all, for C's relation to Deuteronomy must be combined with two other factors which emerge from the analysis. On the one hand, every sign of dependence on Deuteronomy, whether in the use of its peculiar language or in a recognition of its authority as a law, is confined to the Chronicler's narrative. In no case does the reviser show any similar influence: his affinities are with Exodus, Numbers, and Ezra. On the other hand, the reviser appealed beyond the practices which C had assigned to David to the higher authority of the practices which God commanded to Moses in his law. C ignored the late law and recognized a certain authority in the Deuteronomic: the reviser appealed to the late law and ignored Deuteronomy. There can be only one conclusion from this situation, and it supports the earlier date for the Chronicler. At the time when the reviser wrote, Deuteronomy had passed into complete desuetude as a law: but the circle to which C belonged and for which he wrote had not yet adopted this attitude, but recognized a certain authority in the older code.

The Chronicler can only have belonged to the community which had never been in exile. These men, who comprised members of Israel and Judah, were not so negligible as the author of the book of Ezra represented. In his eyes the entire work of restoring the temple was undertaken and carried out by the returned exiles: and the men who had remained in Palestine meekly accepted the direction of their spiritual and intellectual superiors. But the remanent members of Israel were not so submissive to dictation from men who had for a generation been cut off from the means of grace and had lived among the pollution of heathenism. After the first captivity Jeremiah sharply rebuked their predecessors for spiritual pride, because they counted themselves to have been spared in the day of the divine anger which had swept away their fellows. Their successors could not fail to draw the same inference from the heavier chastisement which had visited the later exiles. Nor did the native population which escaped the Exile surrender the faith of their fathers after they had recovered from the stunning effects of Nebuchadrezzar's victory. Since Torrey first broached the suggestion that the temple-site continued to be the centre of a cult, evidence has been accumulating in support of his contention. In my judgement the faithful remnant in Israel and Judah had combined to renew the sacrificial worship on its ancient site, and had taken steps to provide for its continuance. We possess in Neh. c. x the terms of the pact into which these men entered in order to guarantee that the house of God should not be forsaken.[1] They taxed themselves for its support, and pledged themselves to continue the offerings which were commanded by their law. The community which entered into this pact was composed of men drawn from both Judah and Israel, and therefore the servants of the altar were priests and levites, who appear alongside each other and who were equally supported from the sacred revenues. The Chronicler belonged to this little community, and his book was written to support their position. The men had taken courage after the crushing defeat which had befallen their nation, and had found a new centre for their national life. Though their independence had disappeared with their kingdom, they had solemnly resolved in their pact that they 'would not forsake the house of their God'. One of their number reviewed the history of the kingdom, and set it all in a new light. It had fallen because of the failure of its leaders to implement the divine conditions which alone could guarantee its continuance. But it had not fallen until it had created that house of God, through which the divine purpose with Israel was continued in force. God had not cast off His ancient people. The house of God was also one in which all Israel had their place by right. When Judah and Israel combined to maintain the sanctuary they renewed a unity which had only been interrupted for a time. When David had founded the first sanctuary in Jerusalem he summoned all Israel to assist in the transference of the ark.

[1] For the proof see *Post-Exilic Judaism*, pp. 67 ff.

It was the united nation which attended Solomon's dedication service, when the glory of the Lord filled the house. As soon as the northern kingdom had disappeared, Hezekiah sent messengers through all Israel to invite the people to join their brethren at their common sanctuary. What the first great reforming king planned Josiah continued. Finally, no other document except the pact and the work of the Chronicler set levite and priest on an equal footing as servants of the cult.

The return of the exiles saw the issue of another manifesto from a different quarter. The scheme which appears in Ezekiel was produced by an intransigent supporter of the old use of the temple. The only men who might approach the altar were the sons of Zadok, the only legitimate priests. As for the levites, they must be relegated to menial offices, as a penalty for their having been not only partakers in, but active agents in promoting the apostasy of Israel. The Chronicler did not leave the last charge without an answer. He stated that the first sanctuary in Jerusalem was the tent which housed the ark, and that there David left the levites to serve the sacred emblem, which they alone were privileged to carry. As for the apostasy of Israel, the levites were so far from supporting it that they forsook their livelihood in the north rather than have any share in the national sin. They had given signal proof of their faithfulness.

The final polity for Judaism accepted neither the extreme demands of the Legitimists among the returned exiles, nor the proposals which were put forward by the leaders of the remanent community in Palestine. Like most things in this world which have endured the test of time, it was a compromise which occupied a middle position and attempted to satisfy the more moderate elements on both sides. It refused to limit the priesthood to the men who had served the altar in Solomon's temple, and by widening the qualification to include all who could claim descent from Aaron it included the priests in Judah who had never been in exile.

It also refused to admit the levites to an equal status with the priests, but instead of degrading the men to the mere menial offices of the sanctuary, gave them an honoured, though strictly subordinate position beside the higher clergy.

INDEX OF SCRIPTURE PASSAGES
SPECIALLY DISCUSSED

GENERAL INDEX

PRINTED IN
GREAT BRITAIN
AT THE
UNIVERSITY PRESS
OXFORD
BY
JOHN JOHNSON
PRINTER
TO THE
UNIVERSITY